Judith Jone

NIGGA PLEASE!!!

REMEMBER WHO YOU WERE BEFORE YOU WERE TOLD WHO YOU SHOULD BE

An ongoing conversation

Best -
PLeonard
10/21

PATRICIA MEADE LEONARD

NIGGA PLEASE!!!
Remember Who You Were Before You Were Told Who You Should Be

Non-Fiction; African American Studies, Teens, Young Adults

Library of Congress Control Number:		*2021911228*
ISBN-13:	*Paperback:*	*978-1-64749-487-2*
	ePub:	*978-1-64749-488-9*

Printed in the United States of America

GoToPublish LLC
1-888-337-1724
www.gotopublish.com
info@gotopublish.com

CONTENTS

"Until lions have their own historians, tales of the hunt will always glorify the hunter."

AFRICAN PROVERB

"But 'glory doesn't mean 'a nice knock-down argument,'' Alice objected. "When I use a word,' Humpty Dumpty said in rather a scornful tone, 'it means just what I choose it to mean — neither more nor less.' 'The question is,' said Alice, 'whether you can make words mean so many different things.' 'The question is,' said Humpty, *'which is to be master — that's all.''*

Through the Looking Glass by Lewis Carroll

For my mother Rose Williams Meade,
the wise one who raised her children on home-cooking,
proverbs, humor and Black mother's love.

For my sons and grands Seth, Brandon, Bret, Imani, Benjamin,
Nina. Thank you for keeping me grateful and inspired.

For our sons and daughters on their uncertain journey:
"If you disrespect yourselves You do not realize the greatness
from which you came". The Honorable Marcus Garvey

ACKNOWLEDGEMENTS

Special thanks for helping me to get to this place. Your support, encouragement, and guidance cannot be measured

Nurse Fannie Clark, mentor, friend, and ancestor guide; Dr. Bridget McCurtis, Rodney Terich Leonard, Cyril Innis, Jr., Robert Gumbs, Dorothy Martinez and the team at GoTo Publish for bringing this project to completion.

With gratitude and appreciation for your love, friendship, and having faith in my contribution to the conversation:

Angela Suriel, Phyllis Ware, Jill Brooks, Gwen Rose and Brad Patterson, Sheila Evans, Iris Morales, Jose Angel Figueroa, Nyia Eady, Potonia Hampton, Ernani Silva, Shirley Key, Nafisa Cummings, Paul and Judy Meade, Maureen Holder, Carey Byrd, Carlos San Juan Garcia, Anita King, Wayne Moorehead, Mark Williamson, Nate Lucas, Al 'Silky Black' Stewart, Luz Hernandez, Ahmasi Lloyd, Dr. Maat Jackson, Linwood Eady, George Walters, Ella Harris

Special thanks to my family in Ghana. My life has been immeasurably enriched by your friendship, support, and amazing shared experiences:

IMAHKUS Okofu Ababio, Nana Okofu, Rabbi Kohain Nathanyah Halevi, Mabel Halevi, Shabazz and family, Bongo Shorty, Big Mama, Opambea Oganey, Professor James Small, Drs. Leonard and Rosalind Jeffries, Traci Ancrum, Jintz Bagwell, Siisi, Sarah Yitchak, Reuben Yitchak, Janet Neiger,

Ed and Bertha Brown, Adjoa Childs, Chekesia, Dr. Z, Justice, Sam, Ngone Aw, Israel, Abraham, Muhammad, Kojo, Mama Zulu, Sonia and Byron Lye-Fook, Laurencia, Sister Kate, Bernard Saunders, Kojo, Frazier

i. NOTES ON NIGGER, NIGGA, NIGUS, NEGUS, NIGIST (Spelling Variations)

The terms Nigger, Nigga, Nigus, **Negus**, Nigist, Nega are used interchangeably as appropriate to the text and context.

Nigger... adjective, noun

Nigger is widely believed to be a corruption of legitimate words such as negro and negre, Spanish, Portuguese for the color black; Niger, (Ny-ger) Latin for black, and the name of a river that runs through West Africa. Niger (Nee-jeer) and Nigeria are African countries. The word nigger is used by whites to demoralize Black people, while Blacks use it in friendly fashion.

Nigga...adjective, noun

This version of nigger was legitimized by Hip Hop, Rap and Gangsta Rap culture and used widely by other ethnic groups in America and around the world who believe the different spelling nullifies any racist intent.

Nigus (Ge'ez, Ethiopia's Ancient Classical Language**)** Royalty; King; Emperor; **Negist** Queen

Negus, Nega (Amharic, official language of Ethiopia) Royalty; King; Emperor

Negus

noun ne·gus \'nē-gəs, ni-'güs\

: king—used as a title of the sovereign of Ethiopia

Amharic *nəgus*, from Geez *nĕgūša nagaśt* king of kings

First Known Use: 1594

ii. WORDS and LANGUAGE

"Words and language have the power to create and alter reality"

Language is a means of communication which uses signs, symbols, pictures, art forms, and other visual and physical aids to convey a message. Audible sounds unique to human beings dates back to prehistoric times. Eventually, these sounds formed words which allowed people who uttered the same sounds or words, to communicate messages and identify objects. Language has become a lot more expansive since ancient times with words being continually created in order to name and give identity to new inventions and technologies, while the meanings of other words change over time. Yet the objective is the same; to convey a message that speakers of the same language will understand.

Many inventions and creations are named for their inventor or creator. Other words derive from languages which may have similar meanings or characteristics, while other word meanings were arbitrarily assigned, and with continued use, their meaning became agreed upon.

For example, the word *diesel* is named for Rudolf Diesel, the inventor of an engine now officially known as a *Diesel* engine; and the *leotard* worn by dancers, is named for its creator, Jules Leotard, a French acrobatic and trapeze performer. Most Americans and others around the world understand these words and what they represent.

When one speaks of *vegetables*, speakers of American English understand the message as a variety of food items that grow from the ground, on a vine, or on a stalk and are said to be good for you. If we particularize the vegetable to broccoli or carrots, we visualize picture symbols of the vegetables as we know them. We understand the message because we understand the same language. This is true for all spoken languages.

Over the course of history, words go out of use and disappear from our lexicon. *Jollux*, which once meant a fat person; and *brabble*, to argue about trifles, or small stuff, are words no longer used. Other words such as *geek, techie, emoji*, have been created with the advancement of technology. The word *boycott*, named for Charles Boycott, a 19th century army captain ostracized from his native Ireland, today refers to deliberately not buying certain products or patronizing a business; an example of word meanings changing over time.

****

Slang, or informal words historically associated with Black English, spoken by and between Black people, has never been considered standard American English, yet Blacks have an innate understanding of what is meant. Nuance and tone often has a lot to do with this.

When I was in grade school, the word *bad* was the opposite of *good;* naughty; not nice. I later learned that in the Black vernacular, *bad* also meant good; cool, as in, "that's a bad hat"; which translates as *good choice and stylish*, or "we a baad people" which has several translations, all speaking to some aspect of our creativity, resilience, intelligence, and our ability to make a way out of no way.

Black slang and aphorisms are immediately recognizable all over mainstream media. Problem is whites who speak the words in commercials and other media exchanges lack Black vocal personality. When intonation and charisma are missing, there is little energy in the message. Black-speak is colorful and stimulating. The literal becomes metaphorical and oftentimes, proverbial. Black slang is poetry in motion.

I remember when dead presidents referred to dead presidents. Abraham Lincoln is a dead president. George Washington was a president who died. Then I learned that in Black slang circles, *dead presidents'* meant money; United States currency where images of dead presidents live and are very much in demand.

Back in the day, when a brother talked about his *crib*, he didn't mean where he slept as a baby. He was talking about his house; apartment; room; small room...as small as a crib. His *sky* was his hat; and to *ice,* or *give shade* was to ignore somebody. If you got your *coat pulled,* no one was actually pulling your coat; rather, they were making you aware of something you might want to know. And, if you were called *crazy,* you were not a candidate for a mental institution; you were held up as an example of a person who is not afraid.

Crazy people embodied a freedom many of us would have liked to have. If a hostile white man with a gun called a crazy nigger, crazy, that crazy nigger might yell back, "yo mama!" As erratic and daring as crazy niggers could be, (I've known a few) we loved them. They often said what we were thinking, and doing what we did not have the courage to do. They were crazy sane.

Ultimately, what a word means depends not so much on how it came into being, or how words change over time, but on how this powerful tool we call language is used today to shape national and international opinions by creating and manipulating narratives, people and truth.

American History is a prime example of a history subjectively documented by people who manipulate language and influence people to believe what amounts to opinions not grounded in fact or truth. Language can be just as powerful for everyday people who also use it to manipulate, injure and control or encourage and support. In America *nigger* is a word that still has the power to injure in spite of its wide-spread multi-ethnic use among rap, hip hop and urban cultures all over the world. As we the people become tone deaf and turn a blind eye, we're losing our children to the normalization of words and language that disrespects our ancestors and elders and the sacrifices they made to make life more equitable for their descendants. This is the ultimate injury to our humanity and history.

Nigga, with a new spelling and diverse users including whites, now partnered with words that demean, demoralize, denigrates women, glorifies guns, violence and fosters self-hate doesn't make it friendly and non-racist, it makes it stupid and more damaging than original nigger, placing those who identify as gangsta niggas at serious risk in the larger world where nothing has changed. The word nigga is not the real culprit, rather our loss of power over the word we self-defined and kept within our family and communities. It is time to reclaim our power and bring our own brand of nigger back home. We will learn why.

****

Living in a big urban environment, there is no refuge from nigga talk and behaviors which are often companions. Nigga can be heard and overheard everywhere, used by young, old, male, female, LGBTQ, even children who idealize rappers and their music or who hear parents and caregivers using the word disrespectfully. On the surface it may seem the noxious and vile nigger persona created by the dominant class hundreds of years ago has been redeemed and set free; that original white American defined nigger has been neutralized and modified to include whites and anyone else who desires a non-discriminatory, friendly nigga experience. This is a lie we should not accept.

Original white American defined nigger may have been neutralized because of its incessant use in rap/hip hop and many urban communities, but this is in word only. A new spelling and its friendly use in the world of rap, hip hop, and non-Black populations does not change internalized images and nigger attributes in the larger world. When I hear gangsta rap lyrics in this age of bitches, ho's, guns, killing police, kinky sex and more, I hear self-defeating rhetoric and going nowhere bravado. I am not alone in this way of thinking.

Regrettably, abusers of the word set new lows and moral obstacles for a people still wrestling with systems and institutions which already deem African Americans *unworthy*. Their denigration of culture and family values in no way enhances their humanity or their genius and does nothing tangible to further our goal of equality, justice and positive change. It boils down to an embarrassing display of ignorance and minstrelsy; a *hate thyself* syndrome our ancestors would not understand. In fact, it is not easy to understand pants worn under the ass, sometimes around the knees with dirty underwear, and conversations with words that alternate between motherfucker, nigga, fuck you, and that bitch ho. Who can take these losers seriously?

****

The earliest Africans brought to the North American colonies under the British Crown had English forced upon them which became the predominant language of American born Africans and whites. However, because African Americans and whites have different experiences as American citizens, there is often disagreement. For example, Black people's view of American democracy may be different from whites because America always favors whites. Although we speak the same language, we understand many things differently.

African Americans live in 'double consciousness' mode which can be interpreted several ways. Paul Lawrence Dunbar's poem, "We Wear the Mask" first published in 1896, says that African Americans with "torn and bleeding hearts we smile...and why should we let the world know of our tears and sighs"? Nay, he wrote, "let them see us while we wear the mask" [1] No explanation needed here.

Dr. W.E.B. DuBois, scholar, Civil Rights activist and one of the founders of the NAACP, addressed the issue of 'double consciousness' in an article he wrote for the Atlantic Magazine in 1897 entitled *Strivings of the Negro People.* "The dilemma of African Americans", says DuBois, "is that we are unable to fully express our Blackness which is in conflict with our identity as Americans". We have gotten better about self-expression and not wearing a mask, but we could use some help when it comes to not seeing ourselves through the eyes of others. Living this duality is necessary if we are to function responsibly in America where whiteness is given preference without conscience or shame. We wish it were different, but an unintentional benefit is that it keeps us in balance, our senses sharpened and our spirits resilient.

Our genius is our ability to manage these contradictions and continuously create and enhance African American culture and American life. The challenge we must now face in our ever

---

1 We Wear The Mask by Paul Lawrence Dunbar

We wear the mask that grins and lies,
It hides our cheeks and shades our eyes,
This debt we pay to human guile;
With torn and bleeding hearts we smile,
And mouth with myriad subtleties.

Why should the world be over-wise
In counting all our tears and sighs?
Nay, let them only see us, while
We wear the mask.

expanding technological world is being intentional about when and how we express our Blackness. Gangsta style language and behavior simply doesn't work to our advantage. We're so much better than this.

****

Words shape our thoughts and emotions and play a huge part in our understanding of the world we live in. Over time, our understanding of words may change, but there are those that never lose their long-held meaning, even though they may take on additional interpretations. Nigger is one of those words. The truth of this is evident in its centuries-old historical significance and on-going expression among Blacks, whites, and its so-called brotherly love assimilation into multi-ethnic populations.

Here's where it gets tricky. Too many of our hip-hop, rapper, and younger generations don't yet know, or have forgotten that white supremacy/racism is always operating on some level 24/7. Friendly nigga use across racial lines is a hoax without any benefits to Black people who have always used nigger in friendly fashion. Why our rappers, hip-hoppers, and nigga abusers would allow anyone out of our tribe to reference them as niggas (read niggers) is just as troubling as their own abuse of the word. What happened to boundaries which should not be crossed? If we wouldn't call Italians grease balls, Puerto Ricans spics, or Irish micks or paddy in our everyday discourse, any version of nigger deserves the same respect, particularly since it is the most offensive racial slur of all when used by others. GET WOKE!

iii. BECOMING WOKE

Growing up in New York City during the 1940's and 50's, *nigger* was not an everyday word in my household or East Harlem neighborhood. During those days, children, teens, and young adults did not use foul language openly, and we were always mindful of our behavior in the presence of elders.

Nigger was used occasionally in adult on the block gossip generally referencing men who had done something unrighteous or stupid; a plain fool nigger bringing shame on their family and our community.

Like many other Black communities back then, we were extended family who condemned wrong-doing, yet were quick to forgive offenders who redeemed themselves. I never heard a parent or adult reference a young child as a lil nigger or tell a child they were going to 'fuck them up' if they didn't behave. Never! A stern look from our parents or other adults was enough to straighten out our attitudes.

Living among Puerto Ricans, Italians, Cubans, Greeks and Blacks (Negro or colored at the time), everyone got along in school and after school activities. Music we listened to and movies we viewed were free of nigger talk and ethnic slurs were rare. A slip of the tongue, which meant saying black or African, could mean a verbal fight and *friendly* use of nigger between ethnic groups did not happen. Darker skinned Latinos in my community, mainly Puerto Ricans and Cubans, identified as Afro-Puerto Ricans, Afro-Cubans or Latinos and we were conscious of respecting the identity of others. We learned this at home.

Shielded from the in-your-face sinister side of nigger as a powerful and integral part of American life, a bus trip down south during the summer of 1956 exposed my eighth grade innocence. For the first time, I personally experienced hateful aspects of nigger usage by whites. As a result of one encounter, my elders thought it time we chillun' from New York knew what life was like for Negroes in Barnwell, South Carolina, a strictly segregated, lynching stronghold county.

Since that early *life in the Jim Crow south* lesson, I learned the bullying and brutal nature of nigger assaults and egregious acts of terror perpetrated against Black people in the name of nigger. I also observed the special familial, brotherly relationship Blacks have with the word and I will present my theory on why this may be so. But it was the relentless use of the word by rap, gangsta rap, and hip hop urban culture which unnerved me.

In the first place, the centuries-old cardinal rule of keeping nigger in the family had been violated. Secondly, their flagrant indifference to the toxic and foul lyrics blaring from storefronts and boom boxes in spaces where elders, adults and children work, live, and play, disrespects communities, themselves, and the incomparable musical repertoire African Americans have shared and continue to give the world. Nigga is, simply put, no longer a friendly family exclusive. Nigga is out of control.

The influx of highly addictive drugs, resulted in higher unemployment and crime, fueled by gangsta language and behavior, I witnessed the Black experience in already depressed communities begin a downward spiral they have yet to recover from. Nearly four decades later, foul rap lyrics are still recorded and consumed, and the residual effects are still experienced in cities and towns around the country.

I witness after-shocks in young adults who grew up with gangsta and believed the lyrics and lifestyles were admirable and to be imitated. We know where many of them spend their time. The New Jim Crow system recruits victims every day.

****

Two weeks into our summer school break, our annual visit to my grandparents in South Carolina was coming up. This was a tradition for many children whose parents migrated north seeking better opportunities and returned south to visit family. The highlight of these visits was the shiny quarters our generous family members would give us if we told them we were good children and doing well in school. We were also happy with the nickels and dimes other family, friends and church members blessed us with.

What I will share with you is not new or revelatory. Thousands of Black families travelling south by car, train, and bus have had, and still suffer similar experiences.

****

I did not want to go south that year. I was now thirteen and desperately wanted to enjoy summer with my friends and go on trips with the PAL (Police Athletic League). The small country town in South Carolina was no competition for the play streets, trips to the zoo, swimming pool, Bear Mountain, Central Park, and the arts and crafts activities going on in East Harlem.

When I was younger, my siblings and I created fun sitting on the porch swatting gnats and flies, playing hide and seek, checkers, old maid, war, coloring books, chasing chickens under and around the house, and catching lightning bugs when they came out in the evening. I would read occasionally, but lighting was not great in the house, and the flying bugs outside made it virtually impossible to stay focused. I was not looking forward to going.

****

I was always embarrassed and prayed none of my friends would see us leaving our building with luggage that had seen better days and brown shopping bags filled with food for the long bus ride. We looked like we were headed for the country as we stood on our apartment building stoop waiting for our neighbor who was taking us to the Port Authority Bus Terminal.

My father always helped us downstairs with our luggage, but he never took the trip with us. He had no love for the southern part of the United States, having grown up in North Carolina where white supremacists unleashed terror on African American men for sport. He ran away from home when he was 16, put his age up, joined the Navy, and never looked back.

****

Not having money to buy food on the road was the reason my mother gave for staying up half the night frying chicken, making sandwiches, and packing enough for us to eat on our 18-hour trip. Of course, this was true, but it wasn't the entire truth. I didn't know it then, but this trip as experienced by my thirteen-year old, New York City self, was the official beginning of my paying attention to the always present matter of race and racial inequality in America. Before then, I was rather oblivious to the painful aspects of racism and white supremacy.

The brutal murder of 15 year old Emmett Till in Mississippi the summer before was a shocker. We were home from our visit south less than two weeks and I remember how everyone on my block was horrified by the photo of his mutilated body in Jet Magazine which was the talk of the community and the country. Mixed with the outrage was a good deal of speculation that he was a smart-aleck Black boy from Chicago who should have been told the ways of whites in the south especially when it came to white women being involved with Black men, and Black men, even boys, paying attention to white women. I knew a little from hearing my parents talk, but they didn't discuss the full extent of anti-Black verbal and physical assaults within our hearing. My personal nigger wake-up calls were soon to come. Not of the magnitude of Emmett Till but eye-openers to the nigger psychosis suffered by whites.

****

As we boarded the bus, my mother directed us to the back as she always did, and we protested as we always did, but we kept walking and haggling over who would sit in the window seats. As we settled down, we grumbled under our breath about the long ride ahead of us. I was careful not to complain too much as my mother was tired and pensive and clearly not in the mood for aggravation. Plus, she had saved and sacrificed and looked forward to seeing her parents and our spending time with them and family members. We soon settled down and eventually took naps.

When we reached the rest and bus stop in Washington, DC, people got off the bus as others waited to board. Before the driver made the announcement that all Negroes had to move to the back, Black people who sat up front out of New York were already gathering their belongings and moving to the rear. I didn't remember this happening on previous trips since we always sat in the back anyway, but my 15 year old brother assured me he recalled such an announcement but never questioned it. When I asked, my mother told us we would soon be leaving the north and crossing the dividing line into the Jim Crow segregated south (Mason-Dixon Line)[2]. This meant that whites and Blacks had to be seated

2 Mason-Dixon Line; Boundary line between Pennsylvania and Maryland, laid out by two English surveyors, Charles Mason and Jeremiah Dixon in the 1760s. Before and during the Civil War, the line was symbolic of the division between slaveholding and free states. After the war and Emancipation, it was known as the dividing line between Jim Crow south and the north.

in separate sections; whites up front; Blacks in the back. This was America in 1956.

During our stop, Black people began pulling out brown paper bags with food in plastic containers and sandwiches wrapped in waxed paper. We used the toilet on the bus, freshened up as best we could with the wash cloths my mother always packed, ate fried chicken wrapped in white bread, potato salad out of paper cups; lemonade from the thermos jug, and home-made pound cake for dessert. We had enough for another stop, as well as baloney, peanut butter and jelly sandwiches, oranges, and I managed to sneak several pieces of Bazooka bubble gum which my siblings and I loved, but weren't allowed to chew. My mother said it was nothing but pure sugar. We still had hours to go before reaching South Carolina. As I tried to get comfortable in my seat, I looked at my mother and loved her for the care she took preparing our food and packing it so thoughtfully.

The Mount Airy N

MOUNT AIRY, NORTH CAROLINA, OCTOBER 24, 1947.

NEGRO ARRESTED FOR VIOLATING JIM CROW LAW

Greyhound Driver Makes Complaint

Educated Negro Refuses To Sit In Rear Of Bus With Own Race

By WILLIAM H. JOHNSON (NEWS Managing Editor)

A Winston - Salem Negro was arrested in Mount Airy Sunday afternoon at 5 o'clock when a Greyhound bus driver issued a warrant for his arrest, charging the Negro with violating the North Carolina Jim Crow law, which provides that Negros are to take their seats from the rear and the whites from the front on a bus.

The episode caused considerable commotion in the Granite City and more than 150 Graniteers looked on as local officers entered the bus and took custody of the Negro.

It all started when the Negro, Charles B. Hauser, of the Twin City, purchased a ticket in Winston-Salem for Charleston, West Virginia, and obtained a seat on the bus. By the time it reached the Granite City there were few Negro passengers and many whites so the bus driver requested the Negro (Hauser) to move to the back seat with the rest of his race to make room for more whites.

****

Although I had seen White/Colored signs on previous visits, and my family often talked about segregation; places where Black people could not go; and not being able to try on shoes or clothing in the general store or local shops in town, I only thought how lucky I was not having to go through this in New York City. It all seemed so unfair.

During our next stop somewhere in Virginia; I had to use the bathroom which was occupied, with others waiting before me. I asked my mother if I could go to the bathroom outside at the rest stop. She asked me to wait, but I convinced her I had to go *now* and we all ended up getting off the bus. We followed the path where signage pointed the way for Negroes to be served take-out only at a window around the back of the dingy looking restaurant with grimy windows, and another sign pointing to the *colored only* rest rooms in the same area. The *whites only* rest rooms were on the opposite end of *the coloreds* and had a whites only water fountain next to it. Mother reminded us not to sit on the toilet seat and handed us some tissue from her purse.

I remember opening the door to let my sister in first. She put one foot in the door and let out a screeching cry and backed out in disbelief. I peeked in and looked upon a shameful, pissy, stinking mess that looked like it hadn't been cleaned in days, maybe weeks. I became nauseous and my sister got so upset she urinated on herself. Mother jerked us away, fussing under her breath. My brother who used the colored men's bathroom showed up not knowing what had happened, but he knew it must have been serious as mother was expressing her irritation as she nudged us out of the area and back towards the bus. A passing stringy haired white teen who apparently got the gist of what happened, yelled out, 'dirty niggers need to stay home if they don't like dirty toilets' and moved towards the white restroom. I can still see the hateful smirk on his face.

We got back on the bus wearing our shame. Whites who witnessed our embarrassment stared expressionless or looked away, while some Blacks shook their heads knowingly. We were all somber. When the bus finally pulled off, I wished I was on the block jumping double-dutch. Thankfully, the bathroom on the bus was now available and we were able to clean ourselves up.

Mother told us not to pay attention to hateful whites, but I could sense a deeper sadness. My memory of our *dirty nigger* encounter was hurtful, and I knew my mother must have experienced this kind of behavior on many occasions. Although our parents wanted us to know the hardships they lived through, they were careful not to speak of the more heinous acts of violence against Blacks and the extent of the hateful use of the term nigger they endured. This trip offered a glimpse into the stories they kept from their children. Shortly after the bus pulled off, we all tried to relax. This year the Jim Crow signs, the word nigger, and hate for hate's sake, took on real meaning.

Looking back on this first *personal* introduction to some of what nigger meant to white Americans in the south, and most likely everywhere in white America, I chuckle at how I was once so patriotic I often cried when we sang 'my country 'tis of thee' during assembly days in elementary school.

****

During Negro History Week, which began in February, 1926 as a supplement to the school curriculum, we were given a watered down mini-history which began with the enslavement of Negroes. As I recall, from the fourth grade up through junior high, we were taught variations of the same history which always involved slavery, the Civil War, which we were told was fought to end slavery, and the fight by abolitionists to abolish slavery. When learning about Frederick Douglass, Harriet Tubman, and slavery, the emphasis seemed to always be on white abolitionists, and whites who were instrumental in the Underground Railroad network which provided safe haven for escaped slaves until they reached freedom.

The invention of the Cotton Gin which affected slave labor; Booker T. Washington, born into slavery, becoming a recognized educator and spokesman; and of course, George Washington Carver, scientist and inventor who developed hundreds of products using peanuts, sweet potatoes and soybeans were always included in this very abbreviated history. Other Black scientists, inventors, and educators who changed the way Americans lived received little or no attention.[3]

Percy Julian, research chemist and pioneer in the chemical synthesis of medicinal drugs from plants; Elijah McCoy, mechanical engineer and inventor of lubricating devices for steam engines referred to as 'the real McCoy', to distinguish them from lesser effective devices of the day; Norbert Rillieux, chemical engineer and inventor who revolutionized sugar processing; Granville T. Woods, inventor who made key contributions to the development of the telephone, street car and contributed to several technologies of the modern era, including railroad braking and electric railroad systems; Lewis Latimer, inventor who worked with Thomas Edison and improved the filament in the light bulb giving it a longer life; Garrett A. Morgan inventor of the traffic light; Benjamin Banneker, mathematician, astronomer, compiler of almanacs and hundreds more were scarcely mentioned.

We learned Abraham Lincoln signed the Emancipation Proclamation which freed the slaves on January 1, 1863. He became a hero to African Americans and is still revered by some as the great liberator. Years later I learned not *all* slaves were freed; only those in Confederate states fighting the north and that it was the ratification of the 13th Amendment to the Constitution in 1865 that outlawed

---

3 ***Book of Black Heroes: Scientists, Healers, and Inventors (Volume 3)*** Contributions Black men and women have made in science, medicine and creative invention.

slavery in the nation. Or did it? Framers of the Amendment may have wanted the slaves to be free, but they were cunning enough to include the much-overlooked clause that does permit slavery in this now free nation under certain circumstances.[4]

Juneteenth, an almost forgotten holiday initially celebrated in Texas on June 19th commemorates the day in 1865 the people of Texas, a state belonging to the Confederacy, found out they were freed when the Emancipation Proclamation was ratified in January,1863, two and a half years earlier. The reason for this very late notice is murky; however, today many more states are holding Junteenth celebrations and see it as the true Freedom Day; the official end of slavery for African Americans in America. Juneteenth became a Federal Holiday on June 18, 2021.

I've heard a good number of people say February was chosen to highlight Black History because it was the shortest month of the year. The truth is Dr. Carter G. Woodson, creator of Black History Week chose February in honor of Frederick Douglass and Abraham Lincoln who were both born in February.

****

We finally arrived at the bus terminal in Charleston tired and cranky where my uncle was waiting in his truck to take us to my mother's birthplace in Barnwell County. During the ride I decided I was going to make the best of my visit and said nothing about the prospect of using and cleaning the outhouse, or any other chores my siblings and I were expected to perform. We rode for well over an hour before my uncle turned off the main road onto the dusty road that would take us to the house, another 20 minutes or so. My

---

4 **Thirteenth Amendment to the Constitution;** Ratified December 6, 1865: Full Text: "Neither slavery nor involuntary servitude, except as a punishment for crime where of the party shall have been duly convicted, shall exist within the United States, or any place subject to their jurisdiction. Congress shall have power to enforce this article by appropriate legislation."

grandparents and elder uncle were standing on the porch waving as we approached, then came to meet us as we drove up. Hugs and lots of activity with bags and getting us into the house followed. We were all tired and my grandmother insisted we children wash up and take a nap so we could be fresh for dinner.

****

Several family members who lived up the road a piece joined us for dinner. After we ate, the elders moved outside to the porch, as was their custom, where we *youngin's* were permitted to join them. They recounted their day, recalled family events, and told stories which my Uncle Lucius, the main family storyteller and a benign and humorous nigger user, always embellished with half-truths and exaggerated gestures to produce laughter and highlight a lesson we were supposed to learn. My grandparents would shake their heads when he took the floor as his stories usually had a *nigger* as protagonist *and* antagonist; a leader and an adversary who was his own worst enemy. He was animated and made us laugh and he always had a soft spot for the bad nigger headed for trouble, or already in a troubling situation. The women and men in the family were all good church goers; my grandmother a member of the usher and missionary boards, my grandfather a deacon and trustee. They always referenced themselves and other Blacks as Colored or Negroes. I never heard them use the word nigger.

****

My second encounter with the offensive utterance of *nigger* happened at the General Store when my brother and I went to town with our grandfather. We entered the store which had just about everything for country living, including watermelons, which my grandfather farmed and sold to the white store owner. He and Grandpa exchanged cordial greetings and small talk while Grandpa asked for the items he came to buy. My brother and I stood quietly by his side, afraid to walk around the store, having been told to mind our ways in town.

As we were leaving, a white girl around my age rushed into the store, accidently pushing the swing door into me. I looked at her expecting her to say *I'm sorry* or *excuse me*. Instead, she stared back and stuck her tongue out in a bratty way. I got a bad feeling but didn't know what to say or do so I chuckled nervously. In a cocky southern drawl she asked, "what you laughing at nigger"? My grandfather glanced down at me and my brother with a *be-quiet look*, grabbed me by my hand, and we went on our way without words. The shop keeper busied himself at the counter and said nothing. My brother and I were dumbfounded. The nigger incident at the bus stop was directed at our family. This was the first time I was called a nigger up close to my face. Grand-daddy was stone-faced. My brother and I were quiet, knowing we had just had an experience we would always remember.

****

My grandmother knew something was wrong as we approached the porch where she was standing. She looked seriously at the three of us waiting for someone to speak. We greeted her as we walked past, following grandpa who was stepping quickly as he announced that it was time we children learned about the real evil ways of white folks in the segregated south. Our in town event triggered a remembered anger of his own, and he knew we would have to be told the realities of life in the south; realities we might face again in the north and other parts of the country because we were colored. He told my mother and grandmother they would have that conversation after church on Sunday when family gathered at their house for dinner.

Come Sunday, after dessert, we all gathered on the porch. Grandpa shared our in town experience. Mother had already told them what happened with the cracker boy on our bus trip, but Grandpa brought it up again. My brother and I listened intently as grandpa, two of our uncles and aunts, several cousins and my mother recounted acts of injustice, lynchings, and outright killing of Black people who stood up for their rights or went against the code of acceptable Negro behavior. My grandmother was in the house teaching my 9 year old sister how to crochet.

My aunt Bessie, also visiting from New York, told us about the white woman whose family she washed, cleaned, and cooked for who was unreasonably particular. She said the woman was so mean, that if there was any flaw, real or imagined, in her washing, cleaning, or cooking, mistress would deduct from her pay which was only $8.00 per week, little more than a dollar a day.

Granddaddy had a lot to say, having been born in 1885, just 22 years after the Emancipation Proclamation and having witnessed first-hand how restricted and guarded Black lives were; the indignities they experienced almost every time they had to be in the company of whites. In many ways, segregation was a blessing as it meant less interaction.

Many years later I learned from a history professor born in South Carolina that Barnwell County was known for lynching, and was the site of one of the largest lynchings in the country which occurred on December 28, 1889. Accused of killing a local merchant, eight African American men were arrested and placed in jail. A white mob took them out of the jail, tied them to trees, and shot them.

****

The elders spoke in simple language that embodied despair, hope, and ironically, a good amount of mimicking and laughter at the absurd behavior of white folk. They told us children we were lucky we lived in New York because the opportunity to get a good education was better than in the south. The reminder that education was the key to a better life was a constant. Uncle Lucius would always proclaim with passion, "that's one thing the white man can't take from you once you get it."

During those days, this sentiment was a constant in my household and African American households all over the country. "Get your education. It's the one thing the white man can't take from you!" My mother would add "don't mean they won't try. You know it was once against the law to educate Negroes."

When our three weeks was up, I was so anxious to get home I woke up during the night already imagining my grand re-entry back into life on the block. The church cook-out and the wedding of a family friend's daughter were two fun highlights of this trip, but my true take-a-way was my heightened awareness of nigger and race. The stories and my nigger wake-up-calls popped in and out of my mind creating feelings of relief that we lived in the north, and sadness that my family lived under such conditions in the south. The northern brand of racism had not impacted my life to any degree and was not yet a part of my consciousness. What became clear to me in later years is that my southern relatives were doing the best they could, and wanted nothing to do with trouble. God, church and family was their rock in a weary land.

****

We got going in plenty of time to catch our 2 o'clock bus which would have us in New York at 11:30 the next morning. We said our good-byes and piled into the truck. Mother cried a little, but I knew she was also ready to get back home.

Once home, I began asking questions about my mother's early years and what she thought of her life growing up. She told me much of what I already knew, but she opened up a bit more and for the first time I learned that her parents lived in great fear of racist whites after one of her brothers was run over by a train after white men tied him up and laid his body across the railroad track. Curiously, this was not mentioned when we were given *the talk.*

Mother said, it was believed that the KKK was responsible because he was 'rebellious' and white women loved him. Her brother's murder was her motivation for leaving the south and coming to New York City in 1929 at the age of eighteen to join her older sister, my aunt Bessie, who came two years earlier and lived in Harlem. She found work as a live-in maid, nanny, cook and all around 'girl' to a Jewish family with three children. She made $25 a *month*, and had one partial week-end off a *month*; from Friday evening after she served dinner and cleaned the kitchen, until 4 o'clock in the afternoon on Sunday, in time to prepare dinner and get the children ready for bed and school. And, she faithfully sent a few dollars home so her parents would know she was doing fine in the big city.

****

At home in East Harlem, I had little reason to think about disparity and inequality. All of my friends went to public school, played together, used the same toilets, and our families were all respectably *'underprivileged'* without ever thinking we were poor. I did notice; however, that my Italian classmate and *friend* who was welcomed in my house, never invited me to hers. If I got as far as her door, I was asked to wait outside. Looking back, this was active subtle racism taking place right under my nose.

I often reflect on my trip south during the summer of 1956 and how it led to my lifelong interest in racial matters and my work as an educator, developing educational programs for teens, young adults, and adult learners.

****

By 1960, my senior year of high school, I was fully aware of racism and learning more about social and political issues that plagued our society; Black people in particular. By now, I had read a number of books that dealt with our history, among them the *Souls of Black Folk* by W.E.B. DuBois and Dr. Carter G. Woodson's *The Mis-Education of the Negro.* The Civil Rights Movement led by Dr. Martin Luther King, Jr. was a growing force in America, and I was listening attentively to the fiery rising spokesman for the Nation of Islam, Malcolm X, later known as El Hajj Malik Shabazz.

The summer after graduation, a friend who worked at the public library on 135th Street in the Negro Literature, History and Prints Division, now the world recognized Schomburg Center for Research in Black Culture, invited me to meet her at the library and go with her to a bookstore in Harlem that sold books written primarily by Blacks, about Blacks, and if we were lucky, Malcolm X might be there as he was a frequent visitor and wrote many of his speeches sitting in the back of the shop. Having walked up and down 125th Street since I was a child, I was aware of the bookstore but had never entered its doors. Now that I was ready to expand my knowledge, teachers were appearing everywhere.

****

Lewis Michaux's African National Memorial Bookstore founded in 1932, was a community gem. Mr. Michaux was a Garveyite and Pan Africanist who promoted his bookstore as *The House of Common Sense and the Home of Proper Propaganda.* Everyone else called it *Michaux's.* Hungry for knowledge of self and our people, I became a frequent visitor and often spent hours perusing the shelves and tables of books filled with information about our African origins and history. Revolutionary thinkers, activists and scholars were frequent customers and teachers who shared their knowledge with anyone fortunate enough to be in this temple of learning at the time. Michaux's was a treasure and gathering space for those of us coming into a heightened awareness of our African heritage and understanding of the issues during the national unrest in the 1960's.

In 1967, a new State Office Building was proposed for the site on Seventh Avenue and 125th Street, and by 1969 the State was moving forward with their plan. Community activists learned of the bookstores plight and fought unsuccessfully to save this important landmark. Mr. Michaux moved across the street where he stayed until he closed his doors in 1974, the same year the State Office Building opened. In1983, the building was named for Congressman Adam Clayton Powell, Jr. one of our great political leaders of the 20th century. A life-size sculpture of Congressman Powell was dedicated on the building Plaza in February, 2005.

Powell served in Congress from 1945 to 1971, passing away on April 4, 1972. While in Congress, Powell sponsored and got close to fifty major pieces of legislation passed which benefit all people. He was also the charismatic Minister of the prestigious Abyssinian Baptist Church in Harlem. Dr. Powell is one of our heroes we need to know and acknowledge.

****

Harlem was also home to The Tree of Life Bookstore and Education Center where Dr. Kanya our resident spiritualist and astrologer, and Dr. Moore, our herbalist and natural healer, held classes where we learned to live spiritually conscious and healthy lives in concert with nature.

Located on West 125th Street near Lenox Avenue, now Malcolm X Boulevard, and down the street from Michaux's, The Tree of Life, most affectionately referred to as UCLA – the University at the Corner of Lenox Avenue - was an incredibly spiritual space to enter. Crystals, incense, and the spirit of love and true community greeted those who entered. Black people were experiencing a great deal of strife as well as a spiritual awakening in the 1960's and we were hopeful that change was possible. We lost Tree of Life in 1980 to make way for a development project that never happened.

In 1967, Una Mulzac opened The Liberation Bookstore on Lenox Avenue and 131st Street which also promoted and sold books which raised Black consciousness. If the requested book was not in her inventory, she would find it for you. After Mr. Michaux closed his doors, Liberation became the go-to bookstore in Harlem and remained so until it shut its doors in 2007.

Books, teachers and speeches were my early mentors who helped me grasp the contradictions of American democracy and appreciate the greatness of our ancestors and their legacies. I recall this phase of my life with great humility and give special thanks for having had access to information about my people at a time when technology as we know it today did not exist and we looked to book stores, libraries and our own Black teachers and scholars for the history we did not get in school.

****

As we moved along in the 1960's, a rising Black consciousness was evidenced by our natural hairstyles, African dress, healthier food choices, the music we listened to and the books we read. We acknowledged ourselves as a people with a strong and rich heritage who were sick and tired of second class citizenship in the country our ancestors financed with their back-breaking free labor, and a people who were willing to agitate for their freedom from oppression of a racist system.

The 1960's also witnessed an escalation in non-violent and violent challenges to American hypocrisy and her international transgressions. Although the marches, protests and revolutionary activism that took place during the decade did not achieve all of the changes we wished to see, there is no doubting the impact legislative victories had during this period which allowed for legal recourse in certain civil rights violations and furthered our movement towards justice, self-awareness and self-determination. The constancy of political and social set-backs often see us taking one step forward and two steps back. But what is certain, we catch a stride that keeps us inching forward. Black genocide has not stunted our growth.

****

The American tradition of Black genocide continues with rogue police whose uniforms and badges have replaced white robes and hoods. Both hold the same disregard for human life knowing their crimes will go unpunished even when transgressions resulting in death have been caught on camera.

Some of these killings make national headlines, while others are covered up by police and never make the morning, afternoon, or evening news. The more flagrant assaults and murders bring protestors into the streets calling for justice. Some result in clashes with police, property damage, and additional deaths. Usually, after a few days, a week, maybe two, the crowds thin out and it's back to business as usual, leaving anger and festering heart-wounds in expectation of the next contemptible act of indifference to Black life.

But on May 25, 2020, the murder of an unarmed Black man, handcuffed and face down on the ground marked a significant turning point in the call for justice; changes in the way Black communities are policed, and an end to police brutality whose victims are disproportionately African Americans and people of color.

The case of George Floyd in Minneapolis, Minnesota was certainly not the first homicide of this kind in America; but aside from the 1955 cruel and brutal murder of 15-year old Emmett Till in Money, Mississippi which outraged Black people and shocked all decent people in this nation, Floyd's killing outraged people around the world, thanks to unedited bystander cell phone videos and social media platforms which helped intensify a social justice movement already in motion.

Floyd's killing was not the first cell phone recording of a beating, shooting or choking caught on camera; but it was, in the opinion of the world court the most contemptible. Who can erase from their memory the horror and disbelief that gripped everyone who bore witness to the life being casually pressed out of his body by a racist, rogue cop, who for almost ten minutes, knelt into Floyd's neck, hand in pocket, sunglasses resting comfortably on his forehead, as Floyd pleaded for his life and called for his mother. Struggling to breathe, the officer continued tormenting Floyd as he lay dying a slow and torturous death. On later released police video, we hear

Floyd faintly speaking the words "I can't breathe" numerous times. There's more.

During this deadly encounter which resulted from Mr. Floyd allegedly passing a counterfeit twenty-dollar bill in a neighborhood store, three fellow officers with hands on their mace, held back the small crowd, ignoring their pleas for intervention with no show of compassion, conscience, or concern for legal consequences as cameras recorded and the community pleaded. These law enforcement traitors made it very clear - *Black lives do not matter.*

Having lived through the 1960's civil rights era, I couldn't help comparing Mr. Floyd's slow death to the dogs and the fire hoses put upon protestors, many of whom were students. I asked myself, was this killing worse than being knocked to the ground, spat upon and having rocks thrown at your head? Worse that a lynching; being burned at a stake, castrated or dragged by a pick-up truck until dead? Fact is, there is no better or worse. The thousands of unbelievably inhumane acts of violence against African Americans make you wonder who the people are who commit these crimes. No claim to being human can be made or honored.

Almost immediately after the video went viral, thousands of demonstrators around the globe took to the streets in protest. There has never been a worldwide movement of this magnitude in the history of domestic civil and human rights injustices. The critical tipping point we all saw coming in racial politics and policing in America had finally arrived. Not since the rebellious decade of the 1960's which challenged the nation on a broad range of civil and human rights abuses, has this country faced the kind of anger and defiance against racism and police brutality.

What made this killing different from the others was the worldwide participation and solidarity in peaceful protests in countries far away from America, including Africa, Australia, New Zealand, England and Brazil. What could have been just another murder of a soon to be forgotten Black man, intersected with Covid-19, modern technology, and a population who made up their minds to stop running and commit to bringing about racial justice for Floyd and so many other victims of mistreatment and unwarranted deaths at the hands of police.

While participating in a New York City protest march, of all the meaningful placards being held up, two moved me to a higher place of hope for our nation; an elderly white man holding up the words "I finally get it", and a group of three grey haired, sho-nuff white women standing on the sidelines holding a white sheet with black lettering which read "grandmothers for justice". As we continued marching and chanting, I felt a deep sense of oneness. There was a connective energy permeating the crowd.

I felt good when I arrived home after the rally. Before turning in, I watched a couple of videos of protests in other cities around the George Floyd murder. One was of a group of Mennonites standing on the Stone Arch Bridge in Minneapolis, holding "Justice for George Floyd" and "I Can't Breathe" placards while singing about God's love for His people. The spiritual nature of our struggles for justice was affirmed, and knowing that Zion Train is picking up the righteous along the way was comforting.

Black Lives Matter, the banner organization and organizer of many of these peaceful protests, "began as a movement to intervene and combat police violence and injustice suffered in communities of color shortly after George Zimmerman was acquitted of the murder of Trayvon Martin in June, 2013. Today "Black Lives Matter" is an international human rights movement whose name has become a mobilizing chant and prominent signage for activists.

****

More than a year has passed since Floyd's murder and people are still becoming infected and dying from the corona virus, officially declared a pandemic in March, 2020. The great abolitionist and statesman, Frederick Douglass told us way back in 1857, over a century and a half ago, that "there is no progress without struggle"; and it is in this spirit protests continued amid the pandemic knowing the urgency of this time must be seized. Justice can no longer wait.

Although we celebrated a rare taste of judicial victory on April 20, 2021 when Derek Chauvin, the white police officer who killed George Floyd was found guilty of second degree unintentional murder; third degree murder, and second degree manslaughter, we were thrust back into the reality that this victory was fleeting. Minutes before the guilty verdict was read, sixteen year old Ma'Khia Bryant, said to be threatening another teen with a knife, was shot and killed by police in Columbus, Ohio. During Chauvin's trial, on April 11, twenty year old Daunte Wright was shot and killed, and on April 15, thirteen year old Adam Toledo was shot in the chest and killed in Chicago while putting his hands up. THIRTEEN years old! Police thought he had a gun. Neither of these young men possessed a weapon.

These irrational acts of murder committed by officers of the law and all of the other back to the good ole Jim Crow laws white men in high places are trying to enact, signals desperation and the weakening of white supremacy based on shifting demographics; an educated consciousness among the people, and committed activists in the struggle for change. As the prosecutor closed his argument in the Chauvin trial, he reminded jurors to believe what they saw with their own eyes and analyze the evidence for themselves. I ask readers to do the same. Believe what you see and come to your own conclusions about what's happening in America.

Democrats in the House of Representatives have introduced The George Floyd Law Enforcement and Integrity Act 2020 which includes changes in national policing standards and establishing a task force within the Department of Justice for overseeing investigations and prosecutions of police misconduct, among other reforms. This proposed legislature is still pending as of June 2021.

Police chokeholds have been outlawed in Minnesota, Washington, DC, Chicago, Denver, and New York City with pressure on other cities to do the same. Just as the turbulent 1960's resulted in civil rights legislature, sixty years later America still needs more laws and enforcement of those already on the books to ensure equal process and equal justice for African Americans and all marginalized people of color.

Before our long time beloved champion for civil rights, John Lewis, crossed over into the ancestral realm, he urged Americans to "redeem the soul of this nation." Yet, here we are at another momentous crossroads with redemption knocking loud at our front door as the rules of basic decency are still being violated by those sworn to lead, protect and uphold the law.

Resistance to real systemic change is as strong as ever. Some say a race-based civil war is what we have to look forward to. Whether real or another distraction, our responsibility is to stay committed to the righteousness of our cause and take action when it is possible to do so; and sometimes when it seems impossible to do.

****

Becoming woke is an ongoing, eye-opening process. We learn things that we didn't know we didn't know, and we learn of lies we thought were truths. One of the more pervasive lies being unraveled is former president Donald Trump's unfulfilled promise to "make America great again".

The words 'great again' implies that once upon a time, America was great. Let's revisit the nation's history beginning with the 1776 Declaration of Independence and see where we can find greatness attributed to trustworthy and high moral character as opposed to great power and wealth gained with guns, lies, deceit, and greed.

The issue of greatness began in the beginning when the native people already on the land welcomed the new European *explorers* in peace. First mistake! Guns, wars; broken treaties, and theft of their land was their reward for being hospitable. This isn't great! It's criminal.

Then we have the kidnapping and enslaving of Africans who are directly responsible for building the wealth of America. How ethical is it to have workers perform back-breaking labor from sun up to past sun down, for hundreds of years and not pay them a dime or provide decent living quarters and adequate food, and as a thank you for their service, give them fifty lashes with a whip if any discontent is expressed. This isn't great. It's depraved.

Captives brought to North America labored first under the Dutch and principally under the British crown until tensions between the British and the colonies escalated as a result of a series of taxes imposed upon them. This led the Patriots to declare their Independence from Great Britain leading to the Revolutionary War. The Patriots won the war and the Declaration of Independence document was officially adopted on July 4, 1776.

This important and treasured document which declares freedom from the British and states the principles the newly declared American government promises to honor is laced with lies and hypocrisy. For starters, slavery was still sanctioned by the newly declared government and more than half of the fifty six signers of the Declaration were slave owners building wealth on the backs of their *property*.

When we examine the Preamble or first proposition of the document, it states that "All men are created equal". Of course, this is true under God's law, but the white men who framed the Declaration had no thought of African American men and women being created or treated equal to whites. The ruling class had their reasons, but their denial of Black humanity doesn't spell greatness.

Proposition number two states that "They (all men) are endowed by their Creator with certain unalienable rights". Again, under the Creator's law, this is true and the document admits this. However, who "they" are is not made clear so we must look to the lived experience of white people versus African Americans. The evidence proves that this too is a lie as there was nothing absolute about our rights which were arbitrary and largely determined by hostile adversaries. Even today when our rights as prescribed by law are violated, punishment is not meted out to guilty parties in a fair and impartial manner if the violators are white.

Yet, the most extreme and outrageous lie is what follows; that "Among these (rights) are life, liberty, and the pursuit of happiness." If only this were true, we would not be protesting for these very same rights two and a half centuries later. Having rights and being able to assure our rights are two different things. Black lives, liberty, and the pursuit of happiness are continuously intercepted and blocked by those who have the power to do so as Black progress, liberty, and the pursuit of happiness were never meant to be realistic goals.

Black success frightens the illusion of white supremacy which can only be maintained by keeping African Americans and people of color *in their place.* To quote Pulitzer and Nobel Prize winner, Toni Morrison; "white people who practice racism have a very serious problem if they can only be tall by having someone on their knees", or; *in their place.*

****

In 1789, thirteen years after declaring independence, the Constitution of the United States was implemented as the supreme law of the country. The first words of the Preamble to this document says, "We the People of the United States, in order to form a more perfect union, establish justice, insure domestic tranquility..." Sadly, African Americans were still enslaved and were not considered in 'we the People'. In fact, the Constitution, says enslaved and free Blacks were classified as three-fifths of a human being for political reasons. (Article 1; Section 2; Clause 3; www.blackpast.org/african-american -history).

The 14th Amendment to the Constitution, adopted in July, 1868 was supposed to guarantee full citizenship and equal protection under the law. The dominant class had a problem with this clause back then, and we know from experience, it continues to be an issue today. For African Americans, the words *full citizenship and equal protection under the law has never been honored!* Great nations and great people are impeccable with their word.

****

To affirm the point of Black life being as disposable as a used paper towel, Floyd's killing happened before we had time to stifle our outrage at the February 23rd fatal shooting of 25 year old Ahmaud Arbery in Brunswick, Georgia who was chased down by white racists and shot as he was jogging in his community while Black. Or, the March 13th killing of 26 year old Breonna Taylor in

Louisville, Kentucky by three plainclothes police who entered her house – unannounced - with a no-knock warrant firing more than 25 bullets into her sleeping body; and the back to back 2014 killings of Eric Garner, Michael Brown, and 12 year old Tamir Rice and countless other less publicized cases of over aggressive police confrontations resulting in fatalities. Even though we know what racist police are capable of, it is still difficult to believe that three days after laying our brother Floyd to rest on June 9, Rayshard Brooks, another unarmed, 27 year old Black man would be shot in the back in Atlanta, Georgia as he was walking away from an unreasonable encounter with police. And the murders of our men, women and children by police continue.

It must be disheartening to live spiritually impoverished lives, empowered by guns and no shame, who kill to justify their imagined manhood. After Breonna's killing, Breonna's Law, banning police in Louisville from executing no-knock warrants was voted in.

****

There is an African American aphorism which says, 'if it don't come out in the wash it will come out in the rinse." The death of 23 year old Elijah McClain in Aurora, Colorado on the evening of August 24, 2019, almost a year before the 2020 season of killings illustrates the truth of this wisdom.

On his way home from a local gas station store, McClain, a massage therapist and self acknowledged introvert who sometimes played the violin for animals at a local shelter, had the police called on him because he *looked suspicious.* He was accosted by the responding police and ended up needing medical attention after being choked. Injected with a powerful anesthetic drug by a medic who arrived on the scene, McClain was hospitalized and lay in a coma until his death on August 30th which went unanswered, never capturing widespread media attention. That is until the global response to George Floyd's killing sparked a petition campaign by Change.org which collected millions of signatures to have his case looked into almost a year later. It's all coming out in the rinse. Or, as scripture puts it, "the time is coming when everything that is covered up will be revealed, and all that is secret will be made known to all." (Luke 8:17, New Living Translation)

****

Of all of the libelous assaults on African American men, the lie so pervasive in American culture which has caused many an unknowing soul to lose his life or be run out of town, is the classic white woman's disorder; the infamous *"a Black man is threatening my life; a Black man raped me, or a Black man killed my husband and children".* I would guess this happens more than we will ever know, but it is still jarring when we see this egregious act of privilege being played out in national and international media as it did on May 25, 2020; I said 2020 in New York City's Central Park, the same day George Floyd was murdered. Only this time, our white woman's scheme backfired and her illness was exposed.

After she told the gentleman she was going to call police and tell them an African American man was threatening her life, she actually placed the call. Problem was the man was standing 5 or 6 feet away recording their encounter, including her worked up fake hysteria once connected to 911. The crime: our bird watching Harvard grad asked her to lease her dog which is the law in that area of the park known for its bird sanctuaries and bird watching enthusiasts. She refused. Privilege led her to demand he stop his video recording. He did not. She made good on her threat, and the video went viral. The accuser was fired from her job; made a public apology, and swore she was not a racist, and gave generously to African American causes. Now ain't that nice?

Yet another flagrant narrative affirms the certainty that in matters of race, Black people will not be given the benefit of any doubt, and will be judged guilty until proven innocent, if they live to have their day in court. Isn't it curious that 'fearing for their lives' is the go to defense for white civilians and police and justification for shoot to kill reactions, even eleven year old Black boys with toy guns?

How short is the nation's memory that the fear instilled in our ancestors during the crossing, enslavement, failed Reconstruction, and Jim Crow has been forgotten. In a calendar published by the Equal Justice Institute, every day of every month, with few exceptions, there is a piece of history documenting lynchings and other acts of violence and injustice against African Americans dating back to the 1800's to the present. Why is there so little thought given to the fear Black people experienced every day of their lives; from the beatings, brandings and rape to castrations, burnings at the stake, and forced separation of families for starters.

It's hard for me to imagine not being afraid of the dreaded, hooded, home-grown terrorists who rode out at night and burned crosses on African American lawns, or being senselessly attacked, killed or hung from a tree because some 'superior' drunken low-life felt like having some yee-haw nigger fun, or having your church bombed while worshippers are inside praying. And Lord knows, having dogs biting at you; fire hoses knocking you to the ground; and the vilest language spewing from contorted lips and red faces full of hate is scary stuff. Truth is, Black people are constant reminders of their inhumanity and our ability to withstand and move forward. This makes living in fear an everyday burden for African Americans, particularly our men and boys.

Strange fruit hanging from the Poplar trees....
Russelville, Kentucky 1908

What is even more curious about this claim of white fear is that African Americans don't lynch white people; have never bombed a church, or burned down a home, or screamed obscenities at children going to school. We have no history of violence and oppression of any people or any nation. Snatching a pocketbook or a gold chain does not compare to snatching lives and relegating people to a lifetime of living in fear of the dominant class' obsession with guns, violence, and their false sense of superiority.

Whites don't fear for their lives in the same way African Americans fear for their lives. They fear for their lives because of their own guilt over what they have done to obstruct Black progress. They were fearful of our learning to read, write and compete fairly. White supremacists are afraid of African Americans who know the history of this country as well as their own and are proud of their heritage. And most frightening, is their thoughts of Black folk doing to them what they have done and still do to us. Black fear is real and based in historical evidence and contemporary reality.

As a spiritual people, we are not interested in doing to white folks what they have done to us, even if we were in a position to do so in any systemic way. What we can do when we fully awaken from our long sleep, is what we have attempted to do on many occasions, is seriously reconsider who is worthy of our green...you know what I mean...how and where we spend our money. As a leader in the Black Lives Matter movement so amply put it, "be glad we want equality and not revenge".

When we witness and experience the hatred which has been given new life in the era of #45, the truly great and supreme beings in the world who speak out for justice want to know who created these barbarous, perverse demons with ice water running through their veins and who use guns as security blankets? A rhetorical question we already know the answer to. They are descendants of those who displaced, spread disease, dishonored treaties and slaughtered native, indigenous populations. They are descendants of those who kidnapped and enslaved our African and African American ancestors. They are the heirs of those who raped, pillaged, and stole Africa's natural and human resources and claimed them as their own; and the offspring of those who oppressed peaceful nations and their people around the globe in the name of a God they disgraced.

The unrest we're experiencing today has its roots in original lies which have been layered with more deceptions in order to keep the illusion of greatness and white supremacy active, even as the lies are being punctured and the monuments they built to honor themselves are being destroyed. The Wizards of Oz have been exposed.

Finally, as we continue to mourn the wave of killings, people of hope and faith are opening their eyes, gathering their spiritual armor and seeking guidance from our Higher Power, our ancestors, and reaching deep into our humanity for the strength we will need to stand against the forces of evil in high and low places.

African Americans have been down many dark roads and dead-end streets, never knowing where life's circumstances will take us. Those who could not hold it together lost their way while the resilient and determined stood strong, resisted and followed the wisdom teachings and guidance of elders and ancestors. It is this resilience and determination which commands us to continue our American odyssey and leave a fruitful legacy for future generations to build upon. As the old Negro spiritual protest song tells us, "We will not be moved. Like a tree planted by the rivers of water, we shall not be moved."

****

In December, 2014, the United Nations proclaimed 2015 through 2024 as The International Decade for People of African Descent. Under the theme "Recognition, Justice, and Development" the objective is to "provide an operational framework to encourage States to eradicate social injustices inherited from history and to fight against racism, prejudice and racial discrimination to which people of African descent are still subjected." We are halfway through the decade and I need not ask "how are we doing?

As critical as righting the wrongs which have persisted for centuries, is the readiness of African Americans to step into a world free of self-imposed barriers to full participation in our own humanity. If we believe that Black lives really do matter, we must be the best examples of this belief. We must take a serious look at the gangsta persona and the impact of the language and lifestyle and consider if these images represent the best of Black people. Hardcore gansgta rappers and everyday gangstas in our communities are not the majority of those who identify as niggas, but we know from experience, it is always the worst of African Americans and people of color that is held up as the model. My primary goal is to place the terms nigger and nigga, who some say have different meanings, within a metaphysical and historical framework which will help us gain a perspective which will not permit any type of disrespectful usage. We will change the paradigm and gain control over a word whose true origin we will now honor. We know that when it comes to any version of nigger, "there is very little that is new or surprising; however, there may be several old things we don't know" but will hopefully learn.

****

I am forever grateful for my childhood visits south, the hurtful nigger experiences, the lessons of my grandparents, aunts, and uncles who gave us *the talk,* and of course, my parents who came north to escape Jim Crow; made family and *a way out of no way,* and taught their children to do the same. Good manners, respect for elders, healthy morals and values, hard work and excellence was stressed regularly. We learned to co-create along with our Master Creator and Faith in the Mysteries of the universe, solutions to our problems just as our forebears did because this is what metaphysicians do. This is why we're still here when we were never meant to survive.

iv. INTRODUCTION

> When, long ago, the gods created Earth in Jove's fair image Man was shaped at birth. The beasts for lesser parts were next designed; yet were they too remote from humankind. To fill the gap, and join the rest to Man, Th'Olympian host conceiv'd a clever plan. A beast they wrought, in semi-human figure, filled it with vice, and called the thing a Nigger.
>
> *On The Creation of Niggers by H.P. Lovecraft, 1912*

Nigger is a relentless and rebellious word which holds a significant and paradoxical place in the history of the United States of America. Nigger and America go way back; before America became herself, arriving in the colonies with European enslavers and their African captives. Shocking acts of terror against African captives and their descendants in America, instigated by the utterance of the word *nigger* contribute to a national biography this country should be ashamed of.

Young abusers of the word tell their elders that because *nigger* is now spelled *nigga,* the different spelling has changed its traditional meaning in white American culture. Today's ethnically diverse niggas includes whites playing at being brothers using nigga language ad nauseum without respect or restraint.

This kind of freedom may work in hip-hop, rap, and inner city, urban communities, but what I know from history and everyday experiences in the larger world, is that no matter how nigger is spelled, when spoken mental perceptions and images are the same as they've always been; maybe worse.

****

What is really happening is that old stereotypes have updated themselves, creating a newer version of nigger which is more disparaging than the original European-American creation now that gangsta language and behaviors, guns, saggin' and white niggas have joined ranks to help their Black brothers show the world their disregard for their history and culture. Must be something to the saying that 'the lower the pants, the lower the I.Q."

Even if our hip hoppers really think nigga has changed its meaning and its okay for non-Blacks to boldly proclaim niggahood, the questions then become, 'have nigger dues been paid; has nigger diversity stopped the police from racial profiling? Has it brought peace to the nation or our communities, or changed the social and political landscape for the better? And, we must ask, "why are Black people always so willing to share our culture and privileged family information, when nobody shares with Blacks?"

Why whites and others have been welcomed into the private world of Niggadom, and why they would want to masquerade as niggas is curious. They do not share our culture or experience in America, and no one really thinks of them as real niggas. I suspect they do it for a thrill and because privilege says they can.

****

My mother used to say "I can see the handwriting on the wall" which was a premonition; a warning of something to come. Well people, I too, can see the handwriting on the sky. If we do not reverse the normalization of nigga use and gangsta nigga language and behaviors which does absolutely nothing to further our call for justice and equality, African Americans will continue to be a marginalized and disrespected people, always being pushed down and shoved to the back. Abuse of the term is self-defeating and supports the already held idea of African Americans being 'undeserving'. Why respect a people who do not respect themselves?

This political and social mindset may be a factor in the United States government's refusal to issue an official Proclamation apologizing for slavery; or to take meaningful action on the 1989 Congressional proposal to create a Commission to Study and Develop Reparations Proposals for African-Americans. Think about it!

Even more grievous is that if this multi-ethnic nigga was a good thing, why aren't other racial slurs enjoying as much popularity? Everyone knows unfavorable references by *outsiders* are not tolerated by other groups. That's the way it used to be with Blacks. Rap and Hip Hop has changed this. A revised nigga history is being written creating yet another lie.

****

Gangsta rappers unleashed their own *small boy* cries for help upon undeveloped minds who internalized the messages and aspired to live the gangsta lifestyle; a mentality that negatively impacted young Black lives, many already in crisis. These are not the messages they need to hear in a racially divided, fragile society where Black people are the primary victims of guns, killings, and jail.

Permitting those who have no allegiance to Black people or our communities to blatantly spew out nigga and niggerisms and disrespect the residual trauma African Americans experience is a disgrace to the memory of our ancestors and weakens our ongoing battle with forces who glory in our ignorance and disregard. Wake Up!

****

Since the American narrative is rife with appalling accounts of terrorist acts against African Americans in the name of a nigger, I will not recount details of ugly events in our history. Nor will

I offer an opinion on whether Black people should use the word themselves as African Americans have long enjoyed their own fraternal relationship with nigger which is not steeped in white perceptions. I believe nigger has a place in our lives, Black lives, and I will not relegate him to an "N" word. He has too much charisma for that and besides, Nigger is family. You'll see why!

My mission is to take nigga out of the streets and off of rap and hip hop stages around the world where he is being painfully used and abused, a crutch for rappers, hip-hoppers, and everyone who thinks its meaning has changed and that no harm is being done. I disagree. Nigga, like the prodigal son, needs to come out of the trough and return home to family who understand; family who loves him and will teach him the truth of his powerful and royal beginnings; the role nigger played in our survival in America, and very importantly, the possible origin of original Euro-American nigger in ancient Ethiopia. Asserting true Black Power over the word; reimaging, and re-imagining nigga as our ancient original Nigus is the hoped for result. This writing offers a prescription for making this happen.

This book is also a registration of distress and disappointment with gangsta rap's crude, hardcore language which has left an indelible stain on a segment of our community and our musical legacy and is an embarrassment to those of us who believe that Black lives do matter.

It is a charge to those rappers who glorify guns, jail, kinky sex, killing police and shamelessly abuse the term nigga, to consider the dangerous influence on our youth and young adults, and the peril they place themselves in. Rapping about guns and killing police is not smart. They, too, glorify guns; are licensed to kill; and do so in a heartbeat, especially Black men and boys.

As importantly, this book serves as a reminder of the history, hardships, and sacrifices of our ancestors who endured slavery, survived Jim Crow inequality and injustice, and created lives that gave them hope for their future and the generational seeds they planted. It is a reminder that we are beneficiaries of their sacrifices.

****

The business of rap music, especially in the early days, is the business of white men in white corporations whose primary responsibility is to grow the bottom line by supporting talent with messages that will sell and make lots of money. Rappers and spoken word artists who brought consciousness raising messages to the people never received the kind of backing nigga and gangsta nigga rappers receive to disrespect themselves and their people. The money moguls knew this gangsta brand of rap was destined to be a worldwide phenomenon because they knew that Black denigration and condemnation always sell.

Desperate for a chance to make it big, rappers of very modest means grabbed the dangling dollars and did what they were told to do without thinking of the negative impact this worldwide music genre and culture would have in our communities and the political and social landscape of the country. We know who the primary economic beneficiaries are, and we know who believed the gangsta hype and lost their lives before they began to really live.

And now we have descendants of people who oppressed our ancestors using and disrespecting the word nigga with and in the company of their Black *brothers* who have been bamboozled and have willingly compromised their racial self esteem. Nothing has changed except the spelling and a false sense of acceptance. It will still be the unarmed Black gangsta nigga who gets shot and killed by police.

As gangsta language plays out, and whites and academia move in to hi-jack yet another brilliant musical creation, I am hopeful the guilty ones who are still with us and new talent on the horizon, will appreciate the power and beauty of being the *highest* expression of what it means to be 'young, gifted, and Black'.

For some time I have wanted to have this conversation with teens, young adults, and anyone interested in another perspective on the conventional nigger we know and the multi-ethnic nigga running wild all over America and the world. So let's get the conversation started.

****

The modern science of genetic tracking through mitochondrial DNA passed down through mothers, affirms that an African woman who lived more than one-hundred fifty to two hundred thousand years ago in the area of the world we call East Africa is the mother of everyone alive on earth today. She is referred to as the *Real* Eve.

Ancient migrations out of Africa led to new environments and climates, which over time, produced changed physical characteristics; the most obvious being skin color. Africans who settled in the northern and western hemispheres received less direct exposure to the sun which caused them to lose much of their melanin, the black genetic substance which gives color to the skin and eyes, among other attributes and pre-dispositions. Over time, this group lost much of their color and ultimately became today's '*white man'* who settled primarily in the area we now call Europe! Africans who never left the continent and those who left and settled in eastern and southern hemispheres where direct exposure to the sun was plentiful, are rich in melanin and retained their darker hues. People of color remain the dominant groups in the global human family. People who classify themselves as white comprise less than 10% of the world's population.

****

Our ancient African ancestors were the first metaphysicians and creators of civilizations, powerful kingdoms and empires. They mastered their environments and were the first people to honor the source of Creation and celebrate Nature in ceremony and ritual. Visually documented testaments to the genius of highly evolved original men and women can be seen in Ethiopia, Great Zimbabwe, Egypt and Nile Valley Civilizations where mathematics, medicine, religion, mystery schools, and codes of conduct were created,

Doesn't it seem weird that descendants of people who created wonders of the ancient world and mastered spiritual and material aspects of survival would be reduced to a "people without a history they can be proud of"? This was told to bibliophile, educator, and activist Arturo Alphonso Schomburg by one of his teachers in Puerto Rico.

This ignorant remark is what drove Mr. Schomburg to collect and research everything he could find on Black history and accomplishment. His collection of ten thousand rare books, pamphlets, art works, newspaper articles, and other artifacts was obtained by the New York Public Library in 1925. Today, the Schomburg Center for Research in Black Culture is a world-class research library and cultural institution located in the heart of Harlem, still the Black capital of America. The original collection of ten thousand has grown to eleven million.

The growing community of Black scholars and researchers are revisiting and revising histories to tell a more complete truth, making defense of White Supremacy lies ever more difficult. Meanwhile, avowed racists are losing their children to disillusionment, drugs and much to their chagrin, to justice and equality movements to change the world they live in and the world their children will inherit.

****

African Americans are classified as 'minorities', along with Hispanics, Native Americans, and Asians because whites outnumber people of color in America today; 2021. According to the Pew Research organization, this is predicted to change over the next 25-35 years. Shifting demographics and low birth rates suggests that by 2045, 2055, whites will become the minority group in the United States.[5] This is scary stuff for our fair-skinned cousins and is a contributor to the resurrection of racial tensions, whether consciously or unconsciously.

Against this backdrop, of great concern is the lack of respect for family, particularly women, gangsta lyrics spew out. And I'm very concerned about a generation or two that took gangsta lyrics seriously; who imitate gangsta lifestyles but don't know or want to know their history, and who go aimlessly through their barren and rebellious lives with little hope for their mental and emotional recovery. I am concerned because they are so needy, so vulnerable and so necessary in our efforts to change our world.

To be clear, the shifting demographics does not mean that African Americans will be the majority population in America, rather people of color which includes Latinos, Asians, Native Americans; basically anyone not classified as white.

Witnessing the multi-racial outrage and participation in demonstrations in the aftermath of the killing of George Floyd and those that followed shortly thereafter, I'm encouraged that a percentage of our gangsta rebels have been awakened to the reality and fragility of Black life and now re-image themselves as warriors in the struggle. It is this group who come from all walks of life that have the potential to create the changes that will truly

---

5 **Pew Research Center;** Non-partisan public opinion polling, demographic and social science research and analysis that informs the public about the issues, attitudes and trends shaping the world.

www.Pewresearch.org/social and demographic trends

make America great; not again, but for the first time since the Declaration of Independence was ratified.

America has painted herself into a corner. Her lies and cover-ups have been exposed to a generation who ain't buying them. We've been here before, but this time, African Americans and our like-minded allies are in a better position than we've ever been in to move this country closer to its' Declaration promise made almost two-hundred fifty years ago. If we don't seize the time and maximize this opportunity, we run the risk of another round of stripping away our civil and human rights which will result in even more disregard for our lives than we suffered under the #45 administration. Acknowledging the truth of what is happening and what is possible is our responsibility and we must act before we wake up to find ourselves in an abyss so deep we are unable to climb out.

****

America is a nation out of balance with itself. After 246 years of enslavement, and over 150 years of discrimination in all aspects of African American life, we are now in the early stages of a larger, more serious movement to bring equity to those who have never been treated or seen as equal. Since serious times call for serious responses we need all hands, hearts, and minds in the arena fighting for equal justice. However, if we don't honor our own humanity we will never be taken seriously. This federal government will never support an apology for slavery; nor will our righteous demand for reparations be honored, which is the only way America can become a nation in balance; free of their karmic debt, and a nation that can finally like itself and heal from its own generational exploitations and abuses.

As African Americans continue to heal from the residual wounds of slavery and injustice, our basic metaphysical model will help us on our journey; and Humpty Dumpty's philosophy should start a dialogue around exercising our power to shift the nigga paradigm and accelerate our healing of the disease known as mental enslavement.

****

While my interest in the word nigger resulted from my experiences in the south, writing a book was not yet an idea. I had heard about the children' book, Ten Little Niggers and wanted to read it but could not find a copy in my middle school library or the libraries in or near my neighborhood and I did not dig any deeper until I started to gather information for possible inclusion in my book. Here is a little of what I found in an internet Google search.

There were various versions of Ten Little Niggers as a story and sing-song nursery rhyme first published in print in 1869. The original poem or rhymes by Frank Green pretty much celebrates the death of ten little niggers, one by one. Agatha Christie later wrote the book as well as the title "And Then There Were None" based on Frank Green's original title. However, after the Civil War, Ten Little Niggers was a standard on the minstrel circuit, performed by whites in blackface. The book was eventually renamed Ten Little Indians which somehow made it okay for Black children to read and sing, although the Ten Little Indians weren't much better off than the Ten Little Niggers.

Fairy tales and books written for children and young people by white authors often depicted Little Black Sambo stereotypes and other negative images of Black children. There were countless other books where the word nigger was used throughout, as in the Adventures of Huckleberry Finn, which was banned from libraries because of its excessive use of the word. Positive books and images for Black children, like all other visual media is better today, but racism and under-representation remains.

****

During the 1920's in Harlem, New York, the illustrious literary and artistic expression of Black intellect and creativity made history. This New Negro Movement, better known as the Harlem Renaissance, brought together actors, poets, writers, photographers, musicians, dancers, artists, and sculptors who produced works that placed Harlem on the world map. These New Negroes – the acceptable reference at that time - ushered in an era of music, art and literary sophistication with African Americans as main characters and heroes without apology.

Marcus Garvey, Pan-Africanist and leader of the United Negro Improvement Association, a do for self and back to Africa movement headquartered in Harlem, brought a political consciousness and pride in African heritage to Harlemites and Black people around the country and the world. Their legacy lives on in the treasury of classic works, fundamental for anyone who values Black literature, art, and culture and the social and political concerns and debates of that time.

Whites who loved Black culture would venture uptown from their downtown penthouses to frequent the nightclubs in Harlem and 'let their hair down'. The Cotton Club was famous and known for their big bands and chorus lines of beautiful fair-skinned Black beauties entertaining a whites only clientele which was the policy at that time. A notable exception was the Savoy Ballroom where Blacks and whites could dance together without problems. Other whites would come to Harlem, and indulge themselves in the stimulating and poetic life of the creative and intellectual set.

One such admirer of Black lifestyles during the Renaissance era was writer/photographer Carl Van Vechten, who was accepted into this elite circle of Renaissance notables and in1926 wrote a novel centered in Harlem. He titled the book *Nigger Heaven.*

As a patron and supporter of Negro culture and one who helped young writers get published, he was criticized and rebuked by members of the self-described *niggerati* (nigger+literati) and praised by others for highlighting the intellectual, political, and creative artistry of these Negroes who inspired a new awakening. Langston Hughes was one of the young writers who reportedly benefitted from Van Vechten's patronage and remained loyal to his benefactor. *Nigger Heaven* is still in print and available on Amazon.

****

In 1964 Comedian and Civil Rights activist Dick Gregory published an autobiography entitled *Nigger*. He veiled hostilities against Black people in humor and social and political satire without minimizing the pain and suffering the word caused. Other best sellers with Nigger in their titles followed: In 1967 Robert H. DeCOY's *Nigger Bible* created a great deal of press and curiosity; in 2002, Harvard law professor Randall Kennedy made his contribution to the field with, *Nigger: The Strange Career of a Troublesome Word;* and in 2007, *The 'N' Word, Who Can Say It, Who Shouldn't, and Why* by author, poet, playwright Jabari Asim hit the bookstores. Their titles offer some clues to how they confront and analyze this multi-faceted, complicated word which went viral centuries ago. For older generations there isn't much to discover or take away except that Robinson is more forgiving of nigger use among Blacks; and by white people in particular circumstances, mainly educational.

DeCOY's *Nigger Bible,* a controversial, satirical, offering has a different message. It is a sacred book of non-traditional sermons, prayers, and insights he says will free niggers aka African Americans "from limited ways of thinking that keep them from achieving their dreams." Lots of truth telling, The *Nigger Bible* is considered a cult classic and is still in print with collectors paying hundreds of dollars for paperback copies.

The Uncivil War: Blacks vs Niggers; Confronting the Subculture within the African American Community by Taleeb Starkes, published in 2013 is a book that bravely calls out Black folk who became the nigger white folk said they were and have always been. It is these niggers who drank the kool-aid and hinder the healing process in communities where they rule.

One reviewer wrote that Starkes is "one of the few courageous voices willing to tell the truth. We can only hope that his bravery will inspire millions of others to grab the reins and demand an end to the glamorization of the very destructive behavior he describes." In other words, Black communities have been turned into war zones as out of control niggers (niggas) with guns kill each other and anyone who gets in their *me-first* way. I have a similar viewpoint and traced the modern day glamorization of destructive behaviors in part back to the popularizing of the gangsta brand of rap music. This is not to say Black people did not have their share of disenfranchised addicts and criminals; but it is fair to say gangsta rap raised newer generations on a steady diet of violence never before heard in Black music or any other music in the world.

****

In the late 1980's I began to experience a rise in loud rap lyrics and unnecessary nigga talk in public spaces by teens and young adults. Since then, nigga usage by whites, Blacks and others who have been allowed into the sacred space of Niggadom, has been normalized in everyday language, brazenly disrespecting a significant piece of the African American experience in America.

By the early nineties, community activists in Harlem campaigned against the excessive number of liquor stores and billboard advertising for cigarettes and alcoholic drinks thought to be bad influences on young people in the community. A prominent Harlem pastor and his supporters also held several marches protesting out of control gangsta lyrics blaring from store front shops and personal boom boxes on main streets and avenues where children, seniors and hard-working men and women live, work, attend school, and go to church. Angry adults, helpless to stop the onslaught, were forced to listen to loud inappropriate language casting blight over and in their communities. Coupled with the insanely ridiculous saggin' *style* and gangsta rap language, I am still scratching my head and wondering what happened? How did we get to this place?

What the Reverend heard is what everyone else heard who walked down those streets. I was in full support of these protests and each time I silently cussed the rappers spewing out their toxic nigga ridden obscenities, the idea of writing my own book became a real consideration.

Finally, eight years ago, while looking through my personal library, I came across an Ethiopian sacred book entitled the *Kebre Negast; The Glory of the Kings* which I bought in Ethiopia in the year 2000. More than a thousand years old, the *Kebre Negast* recounts the origin of the Solomonic line of kings in Ethiopia from which Emperor Haile Selassie is descended; and is also one of the sacred books of the Rastafarian faith. King Solomon is credited with writing the wisdom Book of Proverbs, one of the most popular books in the Bible.

I would occasionally reference the book, but I thought it interesting it would come to my attention at this time. Skimming through the book, I recall saying in a whisper "I got it. I got it! Words started flowing and I knew treatment of the book was coming together: Nigger; Nigga; Gangsta Nigger; Kebre Negast; Negus; Kings; Sankofa, metaphysics, reimagining, rap, hip-hop, gangsta rap, American, history, Africa, multi-ethnic niggas, and more. My thoughts and ideas were coming so fast and I got so excited I went to my computer and started playing around with titles. Now I had something to work with. I simply had to set my priorities, get organized, and figure out how I would integrate my ideas.

Not wanting to solely recount victim and humiliation stories; why Black people shouldn't use the word nigger stories, or any of the commonly held opinions about the word, the idea lay dormant for years, plus other projects and commitments left little time for the attention a book would require.

****

Starts, procrastination, writer's block and juggling priorities to insure time for research and writing, were all a part of the journey which has finally ended. I learned from other writers that if you don't stop, you will never finish. There will always be *one more thing.*

The result is a reader friendly volume which I hope will affirm your own thoughts about nigger, nigga, and gangsta nigga, or enlighten readers about some aspect of nigger, its origin, corruption, and why African Americans have a special bond with the word. I wanted to provide insights into the sacredness of the word as a resistance and survival tool as our ancestors navigated dangerous terrain in America. And as importantly, I trust readers of all ages, particularly teens and young adults will use the basic metaphysical model to place any derogatory version of nigger and nigga in perspective.

We must be vigilant and not allow hostile forces to distract us from learning and appreciating various aspects of our heritage and history. One day we will become ancestors and now is the time to become mindful of the histories we are writing in our own book of life and the legacies we will leave the next generation.

****

Nigger, slavery, Jim Crow, lynchings, and all of the other acts of violence our ancestors endured and survived; and the love that sustained and bound them together were given voice in the rich musical traditions they created and which makes up much of what is American musical culture. Rap/hip hop has certainly made its contribution speaking on behalf of the disenfranchised in broken and corrupt political and social systems and what is possible when dreams are too long deferred. The arrival of gangsta rap placed the poetry of struggle and revolution on the back burner opening the way for rappers telling stories about sex, guns, and death, with nigga as perpetrator and victim, which often become realities in their lives.

Despite campaigns to stop its use, I believe nigger, like white supremacy and racism will continue to rile American life for some time to come. In truth, the word is so etched into our historical memory and reaffirmed in rap music, hip hop culture and in every day discourse it may never disappear, no matter how it is spelled or what is intended when used. I would bet that all Americans, young and old, have knowledge of or have heard the word *nigger* in their lifetime. Even the very young have pre-conceived images and inclinations of what and who they believe a nigger is.

Re-imaging derogatory interpretations of a term synonymous with Black and Brown people, especially African Americans, is only the starting point of a journey back home. Preparation for true freedom begins with returning to our cultural roots and using the power we receive from our ancestors and spirit guides. When we board the Zion Train, our hearts having been weighed against the feather of Ma'at and found worthy, we are assured the victory. Re-positioning ourselves in the world has to be the next forward move for Black people in America and around the world; a world where running-wild gangsta niggers have no place.

African Americans are in an historical moment. We have suffered many knocks up-side the head since being kidnapped from Africa and sold into slavery and have survived atrocities no other people in history have experienced for as long as we have been on American soil. Yet we rise and persevere. We return to the arena wiser and stronger. We can do anything, including freeing ourselves from mental slavery, to become a powerful, self-defining people. Our coming together to defeat the most racist and divisive president America has ever had tells us we can do whatever is required to claim our full freedom. If the truth be told, we owe #45 a thank you for waking deep sleepers from their slumber with his messages of hate.

Irrespective of multi-ethnic voices spewing out *friendly* nigga talk on the streets and in public spaces around the country, white racial fear and desire for power and control is always present in everyday life. This blatant outpouring of *friendly* impropriety has not stopped the violence or enhanced the humanity of those who participate in its abuse. So what is the point? The point is, it is up to Black folk to stop their own abuse of the term and to put an end to this so-called friendly disrespect from the mouths of other groups who have no interest in the deeper implications of what is happening to Black folk.

As America deals with changes taking place in the world and at home, African Americans must keep their eyes on the prize which is our struggle for equal treatment and opportunity under the law. Demographics are shifting, but will not benefit our cause if we continue to ignore the warning signs of behaviors that do not prepare our youth and young adults for leadership and responsibility in an ever changing and challenging world.

1. DEFINING AND UNDERSTANDING WHITE SUPREMACY/RACISM

"If you do not understand White Supremacy (Racism) - what it is and how it works - everything *else* that you think you understand, will only confuse you"[6]

Neely Fuller, (1971)

White supremacy and racism are terms everyone should be familiar with, even our young. White supremacy suggests that people who classify themselves as white, have supreme power over non-white people all over the world"; while racism is the discrimination and unfavorable political, economic and social actions against non-white people. According to Mr. Fuller, White Supremacy and Racism work together in a global system which is active in nine major areas of people activity:

- Economics
- Education
- Entertainment

6 **The United Independent Compensatory Code System Concept** a textbook/workbook for Thought, Speech and/or Action for Victims of Racism (white supremacy) by Neely Fuller Jr.

- Labor
- Law
- Politics
- Religion
- Sex
- War/Counter-War

Other scholars define White Supremacy as an institutionalized system of exploitation and oppression of continents, nations, and people of color for the purpose of maintaining and defending the wealth, power, and privilege of white people. These definitions are as good as any and are supported by the evidence we witness and experience in our daily lives. Further, if non-whites do not understand this reality, they will be baffled and spend precious time bitching and complaining every time history repeats itself and their civil and human rights are violated; confused that yet another policeman was set free after killing an unarmed Black male.

****

How we came to live in a world dominated by white people, who comprise less than 10% of the world's population, began with myths and fake facts. The superiority of the white race and their right to rule began with guns, invasions, violent conquests, oppression of the people who welcomed them to their land; and their use or mis-use of religion and the Holy Bible. Even after independence movements swept through the continent of Africa beginning in the 1950's and throughout the 60's and 70's, former colonizers continued to hold power, with some form of neo-colonialism in place today. Ethiopia and Liberia are the only two nations in Africa that were never colonized.

****

One of the the most popular myths was taken from the Holy Bible, Book of Genesis, chapter 9:20-27 which tells the story of Noah; his three sons Shem, Ham, and Japheth, and their wives and sons who were the only people on earth saved from the flood. After leaving the Ark, Noah planted a vineyard, drank of the wine, and became drunk. His son Ham went into his father's tent and *looked upon* his father in his naked and drunken state and went outside to tell his brothers. Shem and Japheth entered the tent backwards and covered their father; but did not gaze upon him. When Noah awakened and realized what had happened, he cursed Ham's son Canaan, and all of his descendants to follow, to a life of servitude. Some accounts say God was the one who cursed them.

When we get to Genesis 10 and 11, we are told that after the flood, Noah's sons and their wives were scattered all over the earth, multiplied, and came to represent all nations. Ham supposedly went to the 'dark continent' and is said to be the ancestor of Africans. Racist interpreters love this as it implies that because of the curse, Africa's children are destined to be servants all of their lives.[7]

****

Slaveholders chose selected verses and parts of selected chapters in the Bible to justify slavery, malign the character of slaves, and create long-suffering, passive, God fearing, workers. For example; Ephesians 6:5 states, "Servants, be obedient to them that are [your] masters"; and Matthew 25, verse 26 in the New Testament states, "But his master replied, 'you wicked and lazy slave"...

Of course, we hear what we want to hear and often do not consult the Bible for the full story. Over time, these kinds of phrases taken out of context become what people believe. But there is more to

---

7 **Noah's three sons Genesis 9:20-27**; Shem (Asia); Ham (Africa); Japheth (Europe)

the story; The "Parable of the Bags of Gold", recorded in Matthew 25; verses 14-30:

> "Again, it will be like a man going on a journey who called his servants and entrusted his wealth to them. To one he gave five bags of gold, to another two bags, and to another one bag. Then he went on his journey."
>
> "The man who received five bags went at once and put his money to work and gained five more bags of gold. The servant with two bags gained two more. But the man who had received one bag went off, dug a hole in the ground and hid his master's money".
>
> "After a time, the master returned and settled accounts with his servants. The man who received five bags of gold brought the other five to his master. Master, he said, you entrusted me with five bags of gold. See, I have gained five more.'
>
> His master replied, "Well done, good and faithful servant! You have been faithful with a few things; I will put you in charge of many things. Come and share your master's happiness!'
>
> The man with two bags exclaimed, 'Master, you entrusted me with two bags of gold; see, I have gained two more.'
>
> His master replied, 'Well done, good and faithful servant! You have been faithful with a few things; I will put you in charge of many things. Come and share your master's happiness!'
>
> Then the man who had received only one bag of gold came forward. 'Master,' he said, 'I know that you are a hard man, harvesting where you have not sown and gathering where you have not scattered seed. So, I was afraid and went out and hid your gold in the ground. See, here is what belongs to you.'

"His master replied, *'You wicked, lazy servant!* So, you knew that I harvest where I have not sown and gather where I have not scattered seed? Well then, you should have put my money on deposit with the bankers, so that when I returned I would have received it back with interest."

The full reading of this parable requires a completely different interpretation. As we can see, the passage chosen was deliberately taken out of context to send a different message. The servant was not lazy; rather righteous, bold, and wise in both his reproach and concern for his master; while master, in his greed, knows and admits his corrupt character. For him, it's about the money.

****

Since the Bible is the most widely read book in the world, its stories around creation, human behavior and spiritual values are spread near and far and taken literally by believers. The passage "you wicked and lazy servant", although taken out of context, has survived becoming the 'wicked and lazy nigger' syndrome of modern times.

Old Testament books of the Bible are believed to be divinely inspired by God, yet more than fifty translations and interpretations of the 'word' from the original Amharic, Hebrew and Greek, have been published. There is also the little known Bible created by slaveholders especially for enslaved populations on some West Indian islands. Known as the Slave Bible, this version, designed to convert captives to Christianity and prevent uprisings and rebellions, omits chapters and verse that speak of freedom. Housed for over half a century at Fisk University in Nashville, Tennessee, this Bible which dates back to the 1800's, was on display at the Museum of the Bible in Washington, DC until April. 2019.[8] One of three known copies, the other two are reportedly in England.

---

8 **Slave Bible,** as it would become known, is a missionary book originally published in London in 1807 on behalf of the Society for the Conversion of Negro Slaves, an organization dedicated to converting the enslaved population to Christianity

****

Determining when White Supremacy and Racism took root in the world is speculative but it is generally accepted that its earliest rumblings began in the mid to late 15th century, coinciding with the decline of once rich and powerful African empires and kingdoms. The stage was set at the start of the trans-Atlantic slave trade and slavery itself which established the United States as a slave nation with a majority master class of privileged whites, and an enslaved population of oppressed and dependent Blacks. The slicing up of the African continent between European nations two decades after Emancipation sealed the deal. White Supremacy and Racism evolved into the worldwide system we're still up against.

****

President Abraham Lincoln was assassinated several months after the end of the Civil War and the signing of the 13th Amendment in 1865. After the war, the government attempted to rebuild the nation and integrate newly freed African-Americans into society. The Reconstruction Act which was opposed by slavery advocates passed in 1867.

For a little over ten years, African Americans, including former slaves, participated in the political, economic and some aspects of social life in the South. Blacks served in Congress, gained access to higher education and a growing middle class was prospering in spite of continued discrimination and overall inequality and injustice.

---

by teaching them how to read using the Bible. Unlike other missionary Bibles, the Slave Bible contained only "select parts" of the text; scripture which justified slavery and encouraged obedience. Scripture that inspired hope for liberation such as the Exodus story were deliberately removed. There are only three known copies of the Slave Bible in existence. One copy belongs to Fisk University, and the other two are located in the United Kingdom.

Reconstruction was a pivotal period in America's history and an opportunity for her to do right by the people she exploited. For a short while, it seemed she was going to rise to the challenge, but instead America reneged on her promise and equal rights and protections for former slaves were dismantled. Reconstruction came to an end in 1877 which energized the Ku Klux Klan and other political and social extremist groups who stepped up their violent acts against Blacks and enacted Black Codes and Jim Crow laws that would hinder their progress and keep them in their lowly place. Lynchings became widespread after Reconstruction, and the opportunity for the nation to redeem itself was lost.

****

The early 1880's saw the rise of European imperialism and colonial occupation in nations around the world. With their military might Europeans invaded Africa and other indigenous countries and gained control over their land, natural resources and the minds of the people with religious propaganda and mis-education conditioning.

However, it is the Berlin Conference which took place in 1884 that set in motion what historians call, the Scramble for Africa. Fourteen European nations and the United States came to the table in Germany to divide up the big African pie, particularly the interior, each taking portions of what was not theirs to take. Coastal areas were already being ruled by European powers active in the slave trade. By the late 1880s, the continent had been carved up without permission from the African people and with no African nations at the conference table. The continent is still trying to recover from the pillage and rape of its natural and human resources.

2. A METAPHYSICAL RESPONSE TO AN ENDURING DILEMMA: From an African Cosmology to the New World

"We believe we are supernaturally empowered and able to bring Spiritual forces into the human experience"

In its most organic form, metaphysics is the branch of philosophy which examines the study of existence; the nature of reality, and relationships between mind and matter; substance and attribute; fact and value. The metaphysician investigates and attempts to clarify fundamental notions by which people understand the universe as seen and experienced through their personal and communal worlds by asking three basic questions. *What is there? What is it like? And, how do we live with it?* Responses and theories vary, but analysis and inquiry into these key questions are fundamental to physical, social and cultural survival and co-existence with nature's environs all around the world. Since Africans were the first humans to inhabit the earth, they were also the first *metaphysicians* to respond to these queries, reinventing themselves as conditions and environments changed.

For our ancient ancestors, the study of physics meant observing and being in direct communion with the natural universe, and the spirit and energy of the Divine ALL which informed their lives and provided access to their highest levels of spiritual insights, intuition, and healing techniques. Each generation of descendants continued in the tradition of reinventing themselves when necessary in order to meet the challenges and uncertainties of their existence. Having come to yet another crossroads on our American journey signifies it is time we reinvent ourselves once again. Reimaging America's most enduring dilemma – Nigger - is a high priority for me.

No matter how the word is spelled, or how many ethnic groups have been accepted into niggerdom, it is always people of color, particularly African Americans who are thought to be the real niggers and deserving of nothing worthwhile. Once we reimage as Negus we will be in a position to claim our nobility and status in the world.

We descendants of these warrior men and women may not think of ourselves as metaphysicians as we struggle to make sense of the world; yet the legacy of struggle and resilience in dire circumstances tells us we are recipients of traditions which gives us the capacity to withstand our suffering, and still make progress. Enduring faith is what gives us the will to continue moving forward even if we have to take a few steps back in the process. What we know for sure, is that giving up the fight is not an option.

****

At the dawn of human history and for centuries thereafter, nigger was not a word, species, substance or attribute. Then, in the 14th and 15th centuries, the mass capture of Africans and the trans-Atlantic slave trade began, and the seed for the mythological organism known as a *nigger* was planted.

For our purpose here, we will use our basic metaphysical model to examine this *arguable* term. First, we see that *what is there* is a word; *nigger! a* made-up word with a complicated history in the United States of America. Synonymous with African Americans and other people of color, it was agreed by the master class of enslavers, that nigger would be ascribed attributes and values of little worth and other unfavorable adjectives, which are the deeply-rooted perceptions and beliefs we live with today in American society. We know this was their way of justifying slavery and their own inhumane behavior.

What it is like varies; but mostly it is an emotional violation of Black humanity when uttered with hate by white people; and a metaphor for home-boy, brother, comrade, in most Black on Black interactions. I believe the special bond African Americans have with the word nigger lives in our DNA; in our ancient Ethiopian memory bank.

How have we lived with it through generations of enslavement, Jim Crow, and racism? We live with it with anger, pain, love, laughter, family, hope, perseverance, resilience, and very importantly, faith in the righteousness of our quest for freedom and acknowledgment of our humanity. When we begin to think metaphysically about *nigger* using our basic model, we can shift the way the word is internalized and imaged, regain mind power over the word, and insist upon higher standards for its use.

****

I have found no information that pinpoints exactly when, where, or what was intended when the first *nigger* was uttered, but it is logical to believe that legitimate words such as negro, negre, niger negrita, negrito which all mean black as in color in Spanish, Portuguese, and Latin were corrupted and morphed into nigger. Ni*ger*, (Nigh-ger) is also the name of a river that runs through West Africa; Niger (Nee-jeer) and Nigeria are names of sub-Saharan or Black African countries. N*iggardly,* thought to have some relationship to nigger, actually means stingy; frugal. According to linguist John McWhorter, *niggardly* entered the English lexicon during the Middle Ages, left behind by Scandinavian Vikings in the ninth century, in whose language *nig* meant miser[9]. *Negger,* is an ancient Kemet (Egyptian) word for *golden one.* These are all possibilities which may have mutated into the term nigger. It's all in the pronunciation.

****

In the ancient Ethiopian classical language of Ge'ez, and it's present day national language Amharic, nigus, negus, nega are words which mean emperor; king; royalty; of royal heritage.

There is also the school of Egyptologists and scholars who affirm that ancient Egyptians were Black Africans who were culturally advanced and militarily superior. In the language of these ancient ones, "N-G-R" (Net-ger) was the name for Pharaohs whose black skin was sacred and a direct blessing from the Sun god, Aten. Black skin became associated with God and the Sun and symbolized power. Recognition of the Pharaoh as a living god, and black skin as a blessing spread worldwide to other cultures. The Black Madonna is worshipped in many European and Latin American Countries[10]. As the most photographed and written about country in Africa, the race and color of ancient Egyptians continues to be debated in academia. However, the evidence cannot be denied. Visit the tombs and monuments of Egypt and see for yourself.

---

9 **Losing the Race** by John McWhorter; Preface; The Free Press 2000

10 **Hundreds of Black Madonnas** are worshipped around the world; most notably in Europe where millions of devotees visit each year. Black Madonnas are thought to be miracle workers and Holy icons. Black Madonna images, dating mostly from the Middle Ages, appear in the form of paintings and sculptures carved from wood and stone. The oldest examples and the majority of them are found in European countries, often in the most sacred shrines dedicated to the Virgin Mary.

We can also look at the Sanskrit word naga, which means snake or serpent, a symbol of wisdom, healing, and magical power. Naga is also the name of a semi-divine race of supernatural beings able to access spiritual worlds and Kundalini energy (vital force) and who were considered the highest examples of humankind. Other "N" words with beneficent connections to life and the sacred are the Nile River, giver of life to Nile Valley civilizations and Naghual, the Aztec word for Shaman or Priest. These words are quite a contrast to the "N" word meaning in America.[11]

Most unfortunate and unforgiving, is the failure of our educational system to teach African and African American histories our children can be proud of. It was this same failure that led the father of Black History, Dr. Carter G. Woodson, to write his classic landmark book The Mis-Education of the Negro, published in 1933. Mis-Education followed publication of his 26 volume Journal of Negro History and his creation of Negro History Week in 1926, which became a month long celebration in 1976. Dr. Woodson was the son of former slaves and the second African American to earn his doctoral degree from Harvard University in 1912. W.E.B. DuBois was the first in 1895.

As with all world histories, truth and lies co-exist leaving us to choose what is likely to have happened based on evidence and what makes sense. Having visited the pyramids, Sphinx, tombs of the Pharaohs, and Egyptian Museums, I can tell you, the evidence of a great and mighty Black African civilization speaks for itself. Nothing less than amazing and something our white brothers and sisters have trouble digesting and why they feel it necessary to continue the lies.

---

11 **egyptsearchreloaded.proboards.com/thread/1987/pineal-ancient;** lots of information on this site, including videos that discuss the pineal gland, melanin, origins of nigger, and so much more

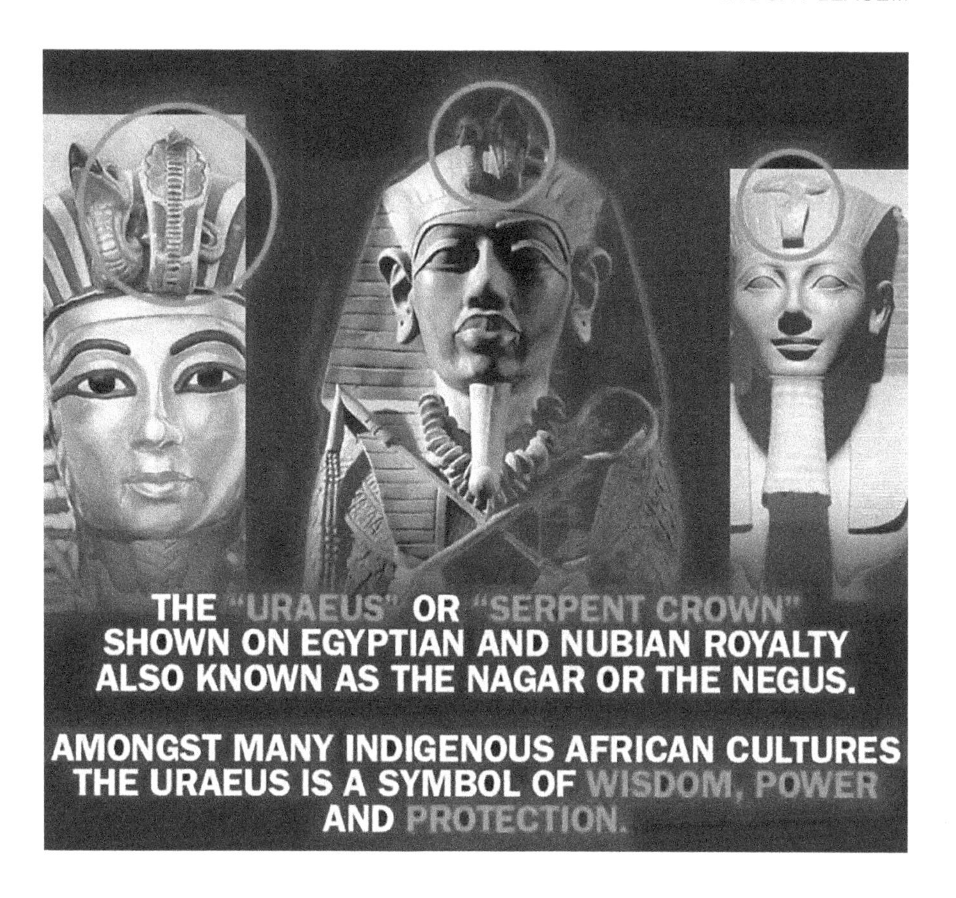
THE "URAEUS" OR "SERPENT CROWN"
SHOWN ON EGYPTIAN AND NUBIAN ROYALTY
ALSO KNOWN AS THE NAGAR OR THE NEGUS.
AMONGST MANY INDIGENOUS AFRICAN CULTURES
THE URAEUS IS A SYMBOL OF WISDOM, POWER
AND PROTECTION.

3. NEGUS TO NIGGER: A DELIBERATE CORRUPTION

> "I saved you" cried the nigger, "And you bite and scorn me. Why?
> You know your bite is poisonous and now I'm going to die"
> "Oh shut up, silly nigger" said the cracker with a grin
> "You knew damn well I was a snake before you took me in"
>
> Adapted from *The Snake* by Al Wilson

As we've said, and what is widely thought is that the word nigger is likely a corruption of legitimate words which mean black, as in color. Another theory deserving of thoughtful attention, is the possibility that nigger is a distortion of the Ethiopian Ge'ez and Amharic words Nigus , Negus, Negas which are spelling variations of the word for king; emperor; or someone of royal status.

Let us suppose that *negus* found its way on to ships bound for North America, having survived the African/Arab Slave Trade which included parts of Ethiopia. Captives who knew the word used it in friendly fashion and it spread among other captives who spoke different languages. It became a kind of lingua franca they all understood.

Enslavers, fearful of secret plots and insurrections, forbade the captives to congregate and use the word *negus* because of the camaraderie it inspired among them. In the meanwhile, their captors came up with the idea to redefine this *friendly* and potentially dangerous word and began using it themselves in harsh, intimidating, name calling ways to verbally abuse the captives, yet brotherly Negus use continued among the captives in private which accounts for the affectionate relationship we have with the word and one of the reasons why it was kept within the *family.* When the harsh *nigger* pronunciation began is a curiosity. In the absence of a definitive answer, I just let the thought sit in my consciousness.

****

As a regular dreamer, I often have fair to good recall and keep a pen and pad by my bed to write down what I remember as it helps with interpretation. Some dreams seem real, while others are sketchy and quickly forgotten.

One particularly vivid dream ended abruptly as many do, and I woke up thinking it was real. I was about to brush off what I dreamed as a natural result of my periodic curiosity around the first utterance of nigger. Yet, the more I thought about the dream I began thinking it was a message from Mercury with a possibility of truth.

In the dream I was on a slave ship. I wasn't a captive, but an invisible observer of captives huddled together on the deck. They were not shackled but had chains dangling from their waists and wrists. The only crew I saw was wearing a big wide hat steering the ship.

Suddenly, the captives began swinging the chains around their heads and went into a loud war cry as they attacked the crew with one of the captives managing to place his chain around the resisting neck of the enslaver. The blue, black, angry waters rocked the ship as the enslaver fought off his attackers and wiggled out of the captive's chain and cried out for help. REBELLION! NEGRO REBELLION! REBELLION! NEGRO! REBELLION! Other crew with chains and guns suddenly appeared and went on the attack as captives fought back and tried to take control of the vessel.

A drunken crew member started cursing, yelling, and pointing his gun at the captives as he commanded them to stop their uprising or be shot dead. Slurring his words, he yelled and kept repeating, WE'LL KILL YOU NIGGRRS; WE'LL KILL YOU NIGGRRS; louder and meaner as all of the crew surrounded the captives with drawn guns and threatened to shoot. It was so real! Suddenly, I was wide awake. I sat up on the side of the bed recording the dream and wondered how it would have ended. Did the crew members shoot and kill any of the captives? Did the ship arrive safely at its destination? For me, this was a futile and frivolous exercise in stretching my imagination.

Some days later I was re-visiting the idea of mental slavery and oppression and ways in which it shows up in our lives and I made a connection to my dream and wrote my own ending. "With guns pointed and NIGGRRS, cuss words and threats of death being shouted at them, the Africans quieted down and did not resist having their feet and hands shackled. The guns and verbal nigger assault worked in taming the captives which set a precedent for nigger rants and the threat of violence as a way to keep the captives in check. This led to the institutionalized use of nigger, the gun, and in time, the Bible as a way to keep African Americans oppressed and fearful. What do you think?

****

Once the guttural sounding *nigger* and all of the negative associations became normalized, nigger was used generously in everyday interactions to mentally beat Black people down and keep them in their place. Our enslaved ancestors understood how whites used the power of the word to demoralize their lives and ideas. They quickly learned to appease *the man*, even when it meant referencing each other as nigger in unfriendly fashion within the hearing of whites to send a message of dissention among them. Back in their cabins, our forebears found humor in mimicking their master's hateful use of nigger as they shared dreams of freedom and brighter days. Their burdens were lifted, if only for a little while, often with a clowning *nigger* bringing laughter into dire situations and providing medicine for their weary spirits.

Niggers were part of the family and played an important role in their endurance. For them, the term was layered. Even *bad*, rebellious niggers got respect because they gave their masters and overseers hell.

****

Emancipation brought little change in the status of the newly freed as they embarked upon an unpredictable journey searching for themselves, family, and familiar faces; navigating obstacle after obstacle trying to get to the promised freedom they so desperately wanted. Through it all, they kept the faith, persevered, and would not allow the perverted version of nigger to destroy them or their ability to create family, build churches, schools, businesses, clubs, organizations, and towns and communities which prospered.

African Americans were not the problem. Most lived hard-working, law-abiding lives and managed to raise their standard of living and educate their children. It was the dominant culture who feared Black advancement and perceived it as a threat to their own progress and well-being. Nigger and violence were powerful weapons in white determination to maintain their physical, political, and economic control.

****

Ratification of the Thirteenth Amendment in 1865 outlawing slavery in the nation led to African American men being imprisoned at alarming rates on false charges or minor misdemeanors. Disrespecting or keeping company with white women was always a ready excuse to imprison or lynch Black men. Interestingly, the authors of the Amendment which African Americans hold close to their hearts, were cunning enough to include an often over looked loophole which does indeed allow for legalized slavery, *"if convicted of a crime".* Get it? If not, revisit note #4 for the full reading of the Thirteenth Amendment.

According to the Equal Justice Initiative in Montgomery, Alabama; "As the end of slavery left a void in the Southern labor market, the criminal justice system became one of the primary means of continuing legalized involuntary servitude of African Americans."

Initially, states passed discriminatory laws which led to the arrest and imprisonment of large numbers of Black people, then leased these prisoners to private individuals and corporations in a system of convict leasing that resulted in dangerous conditions, abuse, and death. While states profited, prisoners earned no pay and faced inhumane, hazardous, and often deadly working conditions. Thousands of Black people were forced into a brutal system that historians have called "worse than slavery."

By the 1900's, African Americans made up the majority of incarcerated prisoners across the south. Today, Black men and women are jailed at disproportionate rates and the privatized Prison Industrial System profits from their legal servitude. Unfortunately, many of these self-proclaimed hood niggas have been duped into thinking that going to jail is a sacred rite of passage into manhood, so they help facilitate their own initiation. A few months in an African forest experiencing authentic rites of passage rituals would put an end to their not knowing what it takes to be real men.

****

When our ancestors arrived in the Americas, they were stripped of their African names, languages, religions, and traditions and taught that Africans were inferior, uncivilized, incapable, and unworthy. For later generations, with little or no knowledge of their heritage, white became the standard and white meant right. Conditioning in this new white world resulted in loss of pride in their African culture and to be referenced as an African or Black became a stigma; a cause for shame or even a fight.

Given the names and language of their enslavers, our forebears accepted Negro and colored as polite references, and endured nigger as an overall and ever-present danger from the outside world. Afro-American and hyphenated African-American led to proudly wearing our present references of African American and Black with a respectable number answering to a mix of Pan African, Nubian, and American African.

The always present nigger now has various spellings; nigga, niggaz, nigguh and any other creative rendering of the same expression, as well as different personas; hip-hop nigga, hood nigga, gangsta nigga, ordinary nigga, and perhaps others which circulate in their communities. This tells me that changing the spelling to Nega and reimaging the term in its royal likeness is possible once it is decided it needs to be done. All it takes is the courage to change and commit to promoting nigger/nigga as Nega and internalizing the concept of who they are. Instead of saggin', how about Nega jeans worn at the waist, and a stylish crown cocked to the side? With Black style, a good marketing campaign and tried and true word of mouth, we can create a movement with the goal of removing obstacles we place in our own way and holding ourselves accountable for our own language and behavior. This is a life-changing choice we can and must make if we are to restore respect for our heritage, ourselves and generations not yet born.

I'm astounded that no one from hip hop, gangsta rap, nigga culture has adequately explained how their *I don't give a damn, fuck da police and yo mama, and the free for all to use nigga they have bought into* translates into respect and higher standards for African Americans young and old. With Black genocide as an ever-present threat, I'm also disappointed that Black folk who share my views have not spoken out loud about non-Black pretend niggas participating in Black genocide right along with their *nigga homeboys* who are allowing them the privilege. When will our brothers and sisters learn that unarmed white niggas aren't killed by police because they *feared for their lives,* even when saggin and dressed in nigga costumes.

****

We are almost halfway through the United Nations declared International Decade for People of African Descent, signaling a time for African Americans to throw off the stronghold of mental slavery and "restore ourselves to our traditional greatness." (Karenga) Our ancestors are waiting for us to reclaim all that has been stolen, hidden, and lost beginning with our history and self-respect. We know that when we really want to do something, we find a way to do it. When we don't, we find an excuse. No more excuses. Re-imagining and reimaging nigger is a task we must take on. If we are unable to leave our descendants a financial inheritance, it is certainly within our power to leave them our rich and enhanced cultural legacy.

African Americans know that whites and other ethnicities do not and cannot know *nigger* the way we know nigger. When niggas are home and not running wild in the streets and alleyways making fools of themselves, they are friends, fathers, grandfathers, brothers, comedic characters, know-it-alls, poor examples, role models, sports experts, favorite uncles, church deacons, corporate executives, basketball champs, alcoholics, and many other archetypes and personalities that make up the human family like all ethnicities who have their own versions of nigger.

****

Writers of the once immensely popular *Star Trek* television series apparently knew something of the sanctity of the word Negus and came up with a new twist on an old trope.

In the Star Trek Universe, Ferenginar was the home planet of an alien species called the Ferengi, who made up the Ferengi Alliance. This alliance was governed by the Grand Nagus or King. Their religion is capitalism, selfishness and greed and they live by the Ferengi Rules of Acquisition, designed to swindle unsuspecting clients into bad deals. For example: Rule #27 states that there is nothing more dangerous than an honest man. Rule #52; never ask when you can take; or #181 which says that 'not even dishonesty can tarnish the shine of profit'. Some of the Ferengi wear multiple gold chains and crosses around their necks suggestive of Black rap and hip hop styling, while the deeds themselves are more in line with the values of white men.

Did the writers of Star Trek deliberately corrupt Negus, king in Ethiopia, into Nagus, King of Ferengi, by creating *out of space* characters who represent the antithesis of high moral values and ethics?[12] Did they consciously come up with Nagus, a Negus and nigger sound-a-like, for the purpose of changing the word's association with royalty to that of criminal? I'm just sayin'!

If nigger and nigga have a place anywhere in our lives, it is at home with their family. Once home, we then focus on our re-imaging and re-imagining protocol which includes eliminating gangsta language and behaviors. Just as we went from Negus to nigger and nigga, we can return to fetch our historical Negus and Nigist and reclaim our dignity and royal lineage!

---

12 **The Ferengi** are a race from the Star Trek universe who first appeared in the fourth episode of Star Trek: The Next Generation in 1987. They and are characterized by an obsession with profit and trade and their constant efforts to swindle people into bad deals.

4. TOMS, COONS, MAMMIES AND MOJO: SURVIVING SLAVERY AND JIM CROW

"Who dat say who dat when I say who dat"

The harsh realities of life as an enslaved human being taught our ancestors to use language, body and eye subtleties and nuance as a means of communication. They understood that when they spoke to their masters, overseers, other whites, and each other in the presence of whites, their words had to be guarded and couched in double meanings, half- truths, and nonsense talk to mislead or conceal information. They used the term nigger when mocking their masters; as humorous anecdotes when telling stories, and brotherly references for each other, rarely losing sight of what it meant to them as they plotted, sabotaged, poisoned, and resisted their oppressors in ways thought to be too sophisticated for their lot in life.

This clever duality of language use and behaviors we may think of as *'clownin'* *'uncle tomin'*, 'coonin' and wide-eyed mammies developed out of necessity. It was their way of appeasing their oppressors and avoiding sometimes harsh repercussions for the slightest perceived offense. But toms were not always docile, coons were rarely dim-witted, and mammies weren't always happy when they smiled broadly and laughed loudly. Their exaggerated *yes sirs* and *yes mams* were oftentimes satirical acts of rebellion which gave them a sense of power over their lives and a humorous way of dealing with their condition. Back in their cabins, they laughed at their own tomish antics as they went about creating family on the plantation and dreaming of brighter tomorrows, which they thought far more important than lifting up their heads in the company of mean, thin-lipped white men. Propagating the race meant more than false pride. If they had to shuck and jive, that's what they did. We should be thanking them for taking low, so we, their descendants would have a better opportunity to rise high.

Another face of tomism is based on Harriet Beecher Stowe's 1852 novel *Uncle Tom's Cabin* - a story about slavery with the devoutly religious, virtuous, hard-working and loyal slave "uncle tom" as the central character.

In Stowe's fictional account, Uncle Tom and fellow slaves suffered the usual cruelties of slavery– and although Uncle Tom could have run away on numerous occasions, he chose instead to stay on the plantation and serve his master and his God faithfully. Stowe paints Uncle Tom as a faith-filled, loyal slave whose spirit could not be broken and who was immune to mistreatment. This is the mythical version of Uncle Tom - a fictionalized story based on the life of a man named Josiah Henson – the real Uncle Tom.

Born into slavery in Maryland in 1789, Josiah grew to be strong, smart, a good orator, and a trusted helper and eventually overseer on the plantation. Given special privileges – he had many opportunities to leave slavery behind, but his righteous and responsible character kept him from running - not fear. His plan was always to escape into freedom, but he knew the right time would come and his escape would be justified - as it did when he was betrayed by his master.

Following the North Star, Josiah and his family left the plantation one night in 1830. Travelling by foot during the night - stopping to rest and eat at safe houses along the Underground Railroad network during daylight. They travelled over 600 miles, finally reaching Lake Erie with Ontario and freedom just a boat ride away. The Henson family was offered passage across the lake by a kindly gentleman who advised Josiah to use his freedom well.

Once settled in Canada, Henson became a respected citizen and prominent preacher, raising money to start a school and helping to organize a freedman's settlement which became one of the final stops on the Underground Railroad. But Henson saw a greater purpose for his life – to help his people out of slavery – and at tremendous risk he returned south repeatedly to guide 118 other slaves to freedom. He did indeed use his freedom well!

The idea for Stowe's novel came from the life of Josiah Henson who published his memoir in 1849 entitled *"The Life of Josiah Henson, Formerly a Slave Now an Inhabitant of Canada"* as narrated by himself - the real Uncle Tom. While Stowe's best-selling novel depicts slavery as an evil institution, she did what all early writers of Black history, stories, events, and biographies have always done, manipulate the truth. Stowe painted Henson as a happy and faithful servant content to live out his life on the plantation serving his ruthless master. Uncle Tom's hatred of slavery and his often rebellious nature was omitted while his deep religious beliefs accounted for his happy and docile temperament instead of his integrity and courage.

Over time, Uncle Tom became a derogatory reference for Blacks who are thought to care more about pleasing whites than acting on behalf of African-American interests. The character of the real Uncle Tom was overshadowed by a largely false narrative which we ourselves have internalized.

****

House slaves lived in the big house with their masters to always be available to serve their needs and usually enjoyed a higher status than those who worked in the fields. Often exuding an air of superiority over the field workers, they were likely to be the offspring or concubines of white masters. They were the original *uppity niggers.*

There were certainly submissive Toms and Tomasinas among house servants, as well as rebels who spit in the pots; plotted against their masters and helped with the escape of those who made up their minds to leave slavery behind. Those who could bow no more, led revolts and insurrections, escaped north and to Canada on the Underground Railroad, or ran away and established Maroon communities from New Orleans to Florida, up the east coast to New York, and lived free.[13]

Captives in the big house with *benevolent* masters had a better chance of learning to read and write than their brothers and sisters in the fields. The book was usually the Bible, and passages chosen for reading lessons were those that justified their enslavement. Ephesians 6:5, "Slaves, obey your earthly masters with respect and fear" was one of the main verses taught.

Itinerant free Black preachers who moved from town to town focused on parts in the sacred text which spoke to the experiences of the enslaved; exile, suffering, promise, redemption, miracles and freedom. Those who could not read learned scriptures at church, prayer meetings, Bible study, and an each one teach one system of learning. They held Bible stories of great wonders and miracles close in their hearts where they found peace. Our ancestors realized that the religion the master class disgraced yet forced

13 **Maroons of Jamaica** are the earliest enslaved Africans who fought an 80-year battle, defeating the British Army and being established as a self-governing citizenry in the New World in 1738-1739 where no other Africans enjoyed such autonomy.

upon them was a curious paradox which required them to overlook the contradictions of religion and slavery intimately co-existing.

For example, the Old Testament book of Exodus describes the cruel bondage of the Israelites in Egypt; their journey through the wilderness and the Red Sea into divine deliverance. This spoke directly to the experiences of the enslaved, their journey across the ocean and their hope that they, too, would be divinely delivered from slavery just as Daniel was delivered from the lion's den.

One of the most beloved Bible stories is recorded in the Old Testament Book of Job, a righteous servant of God who suffers great loss and through it all, never curses God or loses his faith. In time Job is restored to prosperity, happiness and long life. Other favorites are the walls of Jericho tumbling down allowing access to the Promised Land and Jonah being released from the belly of the whale. Then there are the greatest miracles of all; the creation of the world, and the resurrection of Jesus Christ from the dead.[14]

These stories helped our ancestors 'keep the faith' while waiting for their own miracle and strengthened their belief in God and His power to change things if they continued to *"walk by faith, and not by sight."* The Bible supported their conviction that the righteous would be rewarded and evildoers punished.

This was and is powerful stuff. But it was the less clearly articulated African derived supernatural traditions practiced by individuals with no sacred text or religious infrastructure who held their own brand of power. These folk practitioners were known as hoodoo *doctors,* conjurers, root workers, and Mojo and JuJu specialists. In the Gullah Geechee islands and low country of South Carolina, folk practitioners with names such as Dr. Eagle, Dr. Bug, and the legendary Dr. Buzzard were consulted when seekers could not wait upon the Lord.

---

14 **Miracles in the Bible**: Book of Job; 1-42; Daniel in Lions Den; Daniel, chap 6; Jericho Wall; Joshua 6; 16-23 – Easter Sunday-Christ arose from the dead

Followers of these *magico*-practices believed that natural laws could be manipulated to produce supernatural results, or magic. They believed these *doctors* had the power and ability to *fix* people and situations. Whether perceived or authentic, these practitioners were the baddest niggers on the plantation. They trusted the effective application of the African Holy Ghost and the power of spirit to bring about desired results.

****

The end of the Civil War and the ratification of the 13th Amendment to the Constitution in 1865, were hopeful indicators of better times ahead. The Freedman's Bureau was established to assist former slaves with some of the problems they faced and promised them tracts of land abandoned during the war along the coasts of South Carolina and Georgia as well as two mules to help them work the land. Their future was looking brighter in this attempt to reconstruct and repair the nation after the ravages of war. We entered the period known as the Reconstruction Era.

Months after the ratification of the 13th Amendment, President Lincoln was assassinated. Vice-President Andrew Johnson became president, and almost immediately ordered the Freedman's Bureau to return the land back to plantation owners. Our ancestors never received the forty acres of land and the two mules they were promised. The trade-off was that the Civil Rights Act of 1866 passed without Johnson's support.

The Civil Rights Act granted Blacks the right to sue; serve on juries, and to buy, sell, and inherit property. However, social rights and equal access to public facilities were not included. Two years later, the Fourteenth Amendment was passed which guaranteed full U.S. citizenship, and in 1870, the 15th Amendment was ratified which granted African American men the right to vote. Women gained voting rights when the 19th Amendment to the Constitution became law in 1920.

Nevertheless, even with laws on the books including the Voting Rights Act of 1965 which offers protection from age old racist traditions that denied African Americans their right to vote, violations persist and additional amendments have been necessary to update and strengthen voting rights. The John Lewis Voting Rights Act, introduced in 2019, has not been acted upon and still sits in Congress.

****

After more than a decade of Black political and social progress, it became clear that the country's white supremacists would prevail. Politicians were more concerned with bringing the country together than protecting the rights of African Americans. Reconstruction came to an end in 1877 followed by the most humiliating and disheartening period in American history – the era of Jim Crow. Segregation, discrimination, and nigger figured prominently in everything that was going on politically, socially, and economically to aggravate and stop African American advancement.

The original Jim Crow was a white minstrel entertainer in black-face, dancing and singing for white audiences throughout the 1830's and 40's. He re-emerged in the 1880's as strict laws that made equal treatment of Blacks and whites illegal.

Whites only - colored only signage was prominent throughout the south. The north was no utopia, as segregation and discrimination was practiced openly without obvious signage. In fact, the entire country, with few exceptions, discriminated against Black people. Negroes knew their place and for the most part stayed within their prescribed limitations. Most were industrious, God-fearing, and committed to self and racial pride. They believed these were the attributes that, in time, would make them acceptable in the eyes of the ruling class; and once accepted the doors of opportunity and mutual respect, peace and harmony between the races would result. They believed this!!! In truth; however, the more our ancestors prospered, the more intimidation they suffered.

The 1914 release of D.W. Griffith's silent movie, Birth of a Nation, re-ignited the Ku Klux Klan and white supremacy groups who burned crosses and beat up on African Americans for sport without fear of prosecution. This was a loathsome and frightening period and one of extreme violence instigated by the word nigger and escalated by Black prosperity and Jim Crow laws.

****

In 1921, the town of Greenwood in Tulsa, Oklahoma, was burned to the ground by whites. Said to be the worst riot in America's history, it clearly documents the envy whites held for Negroes who recycled their money and practiced all seven Kwanzaa principles to build their prosperous community.[15] Hundreds of people were killed, as whites burned businesses, churches, restaurants, grocery stores,

---

15 Kwanzaa Principles(Nguzo Saba):

Umoja ; Unity - To strive for and maintain unity in the family, community, nation and race.

Kuchichagulia; Self Determination - To define ourselves, name ourselves, create for ourselves and speak for ourselves.

Ujamaa;Cooperative Economics - To build and maintain our own stores, shops, and other businesses and to profit from them together.

Ujima; Collective Work and Responsibility - To build and maintain our community together, and make our brother's and sister's problems our problems and to solve them together.

Nia; Purpose - To make our collective vocation the building and developing of our community in order to restore our people to their traditional greatness.

Kuumba; Creativity - To do always as much as we can, in the way we can, in order to leave our community more beautiful and beneficial than we inherited it.

Imani; Faith - To believe with all our heart in our people, our parents, our teachers, our leaders, and the righteousness and victory of our struggle.

movie theatres, a hospital, bank, post office, schools, libraries, and most of what these industrious Black people had built and created. The damage was so great, the town once known as the Black Wall Street and Little Africa, never recovered. A lawsuit filed against the state of Oklahoma for reparations on behalf of survivors or their descendants went unanswered and to date, no compensation has been paid. Before his death, Johnny Cochran of O.J. Simpson fame was one of the attorneys for the surviving descendants.

Rosewood, Florida; Mound Bayou, Mississippi, and many other towns where Blacks lived in peace and prosperity, were sabotaged by envious whites instigated by fake news of Black men wrongdoings.

Jim Crow ruled with an iron fist until the Civil Rights Acts of 1964, 65, and 68 made racial, gender, housing, and voting discrimination illegal. Signs which designated separate public toilets, water fountains, and other facilities were removed but these new laws were often disregarded and opposition to integration remained firmly in place. Unfortunately, and I suppose inevitably, living in a world where Blacks always had to get back, white definitions of ourselves set in. This psychology told some of us that since whites were always favored over Blacks they must warrant the preferential treatment they automatically receive.

Many Blacks began to dishonor themselves for not being white; compromising values and falling to white supremacy and institutionalized racism, having never developed the coping skills needed to exist under the pressure of being Black in a nation dominated by uneasy white men. These are the ones who have been conned and can't seem to crack the code. They fall through the cracks every day; ripe for the mass incarceration version of slavery.

****

Statistics tell us that between 1882 and 1968, almost 3,500 Blacks were lynched in the United States. I don't think we can ever know how many were not recorded; how many shot, burned, dragged, castrated, or like Emmett Till, mutilated beyond recognition and dumped in the river. Those of us who watch news reports know that racial violence in America remains a constant threat.[16] R*ea*l Negas understand institutionalized racism yet respond in ways that move them forward. Hundreds of years of assaults on Black humanity have not shut us down. We rise again and again.

I suspect whites fear allowing African Americans to fully express themselves without obstacles, will expose their innate feelings of inferiority. Why else would they do the things they do; have an obsession with power and greed, and continue to deny their history of oppression and violence. Fact is Black and white people vibrate at different energetic frequencies. We don't need to be scientists to see this with our own eyes. The evidence is clear. Simply compare the rhythmic energy in Black dance, music, language, style, sports, and just walking down the street. And, when allowed to compete fairly, we rise to the top, set records, and accomplish never been done before great things. The energy Black people exude is powerful; sensual, and desirable. Just imagine if the playing field was equal.

The abundance of melanin in dark skin is said to give African Americans a special energetic and rhythmic connection to the universe. We have proven our capacity to be long suffering and still exhibit a non-violent spiritual and moral core. We who believe in the wisdom of our ancestors and spirit guides know that earthly human behavior will at some point encounter divine, spiritual law. Could that time be approaching? Come on board gangstas. Bring your messages of love and nation building to the struggle. We need your genius.

---

16 From 1882 and 1968, almost 3,500 Blacks were lynched in the United States. https://www.naacp.org/history-of-lynchings/ To learn more about lynching in the United States visit the Equal Justice Institute at www.eji.org

5. JOURNEY TO HIGHER GROUND

"Your branches only reach high if your roots go deep."

Reconstruction was overturned in 1877 and the protections for African Americans under the Act were quickly dismantled. Any pretense of working towards an equal and just society got lost in a renewed meanness sweeping through the country. And if any doubt existed regarding the nation's intention, the significant rise in lynchings made it clear domestic terrorism against Blacks was becoming even more perilous than enslavement. Nigger was likely the last word heard before being hung from a tree to the satisfaction of hangmen and amusement of on-lookers, including children watching in awe and learning from their parents, neighbors, clergy, and corrupt politicians how to be inhumane and violent.

Spectator lynchings were public and open to anyone who wished to attend. Photos were made into postcards which were sent to friends and kept as souvenirs. A hanging was like attending a fun social event. This is one aspect of American history we should never allow to be erased, minimized or disrespected by others or ourselves.

Nigger and all that it came to signify is directly implicated in the creation of dangerous boundaries between Blacks and whites and the different perspectives each group holds on American democracy. Yet, the uncensored use of this word, still offensive for many Blacks no matter how it is spelled, has become commonplace and used without reverence by Blacks, whites, Hispanics, Asians, and others, who are not constrained by ancestral guilt or overt racist intentions.

One of the most alarming nigga fashion statements is the ridiculous, self-denigrating and just plain stupid *saggin'* (niggas spelled backwards), which sometimes have wearers with their pants around their knees, and unapologetically exposed asses and funky underwear!!! Phew! The word is that this style originated in jailhouses and is associated with sexual messages. Ironically, I first thought the style was a message for the police, like, "see, I didn't do nothing. I can't even run".

As creators of fashion trends, saggin' is a great disappointment to Black people who care about appearances and the images that will be photographed and documented in the annals of history. I am concerned about the stories that glorify gangsta nigga lifestyles and how our come-of-age niggas will internalize this period in their lives, if they live long enough to reflect back on this time.

I feel a deep sadness when I see the display of values that makes me uneasy about their future and healthy survival. I may be ole school and I'm not counting anyone's money, but I cannot understand toddlers in strollers with three hundred dollar sneakers on their growing feet. Besides, who can be taken seriously wearing pants around their knees, and a nigga dis, nigga dat communications style?

****

Ignorance of ourselves and our history presents an enormous challenge for those unable to spiritually reconcile with the ghosts of slavery and its residual effects. Thanks to the growing numbers of Black scholars, educators and writers telling our truths, we now have access to more accurate and inclusive histories which makes ignorance a choice.

****

I agree with rapper sentiments that we can make words mean what we want them to mean. Black people did that long before gangsta when we took some of the sting out of the white man's nigger and made him our brother. But the question Humpty asks is "who is to be master.[17]

When African Americans were enslaved and later lived under Jim Crow law and segregation, white folk were clearly masters of the word which they wielded like a powerful weapon all over the country. Blacks were masters of their Black on Black nigger use which was generally friendly, but it wasn't powerful enough to keep them from responding violently when whites hatefully uttered the word. Lives have been lost as a result of losing our cool, and thus, our power. Reimaging nigger, evicting whites and other non-Blacks from Niggadom, and setting higher standards for its use by Blacks will solve this issue.

Up until the popularization of the hip hop, gangsta rap era in the 1980's, nigger lived in separate worlds; the white world and the Black world. It transitioned from whites using it to negatively reference Blacks in their face out loud whenever they felt like it,

---

17 "But 'glory doesn't mean 'a nice knock-down argument,'" Alice objected. "When I use a word,' Humpty Dumpty said in rather a scornful tone, 'it means just what I choose it to mean — neither more nor less.' 'The question is,' said Alice, 'whether you can make words mean so many different things.' 'The question is,' said Humpty Dumpty, *'which is to be master — that's all.'"*

Through the Looking Glass by Lewis Carroll

to Blacks fighting back and not permitting such blatant and open disrespect.

This did not stop white nigger usage, except now it was behind closed doors and in their living room parlors out of hearing by their targets. If whites or any other non-Black ignored this protocol, trouble was likely. Blacks kept nigger among themselves; in the family, in their communities and have always felt it was okay for them to use the term in brotherly fashion.

When we moved from nigger to nigga, we moved away from its history and extended use of a friendly, brother nigga to other ethnic groups foolishly thinking times had changed and the meaning of nigga had changed. Now this multi-ethnic embrace is unrestrained and nigga is running wild in the streets; with no purpose or positive effect.

These multi-ethnic, he's my brotha nigga wiggas have been allowed to infiltrate aspects of Black life without bringing anything worthwhile or nourishing to the Black side of the table. There is no interest in *really* being niggas, rather an exercise in privilege and power and the ability to emulate Blacks who don't know or care about their own history and legacy. The real beneficiaries of this out of control nigga are the corporate moguls who hold the rap music and hip-hop culture purse strings with few exceptions.

Shifting the power dynamic will only happen when we clean nigga up and bring him home to our ancestral teachings, philosophies and our African Holy Ghost power. This is when wiggas will depart Niggadom in a hurry and write unflattering books about their wayward adventures as a nigga.

****

When our prodigal sons and daughters come to fully appreciate their genius and the sacrifices of our ancestors that made it possible for them to express their genius, they will understand their gifts need to be used to help lift our racial self-esteem and participate smartly in life. Nigga rebels without a cause going mindlessly about their hip-hop day with their asses hanging out will come to know what our ancestors knew; rebellion meant survival, procreation, family, education, and achievement. Learning to read was a meaningful act of rebellion.

Men who held the highest office in this nation also held slaves, and all were likely white supremacists. Woodrow Wilson, the 28th President who served from 1913-1921 had no reservation about screening the racially provocative film *Birth of a Nation* in the White House and publicly declare it was like "writing history with lightning".

Based on two historical novels by Thomas Dixon; *The Clansman, An Historical Romance of the Ku Klux Klan* (1905) and *The Leopard's Spots: A Romance of the White Man's Burden (1902), Birth of Nation*, a silent film by D. W. Griffith, was billed as a masterpiece because of its supposed cinematic technique. The film tells the story of the Civil War and Reconstruction and shows powerful images of Blacks as coons, brutes, and would be rapists. African American men serving in Congress during the Reconstruction period are depicted in a scene as chicken-eating, liquor drinking, buffoons. Enough said!

In spite of protests and demonstrations led by the National Association for the Advancement of Colored People, the film premiered in Los Angeles in February, 1915, and opened to enthusiastic whites in Boston on April 17, 1915. While African Americans protested, thousands of whites in cities around the nation flocked to see the film. Considered one of the most controversial movies ever produced, *Birth of a Nation* is acknowledged as an American classic and has the distinction of being the first film shown in the White House.

A century later, another film entitled *Birth of a Nation* was directed by African American Nate Parker. This 2016 version tells the story of Nat Turner, a slave who made history when he led an insurrection in Southampton, Virginia in 1831 where more than sixty whites were killed. Turner evaded authorities for several months but was eventually captured and hanged. The state also executed 56 Blacks and militias killed at least 100 Blacks, slave and free, most of whom were not involved in the rebellion. Parker posits Turner as a hero who decided to do something radical about his condition of enslavement.

Books have been written about Turner's rebellion, primarily by whites from their subjective point of view. Turner's white lawyer, T.R. Gray, claims that while Turner was in prison awaiting his fate, he gave him an account of his life and what motivated him. No one can verify the authenticity of Gray's account which suggests that Turner saw himself as a prophet to whom God gave visions and signs that inspired his revolt. All other accounts of Turner's life and motivation, including William Styron's 1967 Pulitzer Prize winning book, Confessions of Nat Turner, are speculative at best. Turner was born in 1800 and died at the age of 31.

****

One of the earliest and largest slave revolts occurred on September 9, 1739 in Charleston, South Carolina near the Stono River. Also known as Cato's Conspiracy, rebels joined Cato as they marched to a firearms store, killed the shopkeepers and armed themselves. Led by native Africans who spoke Portuguese and likely were from the Central African Kingdom of Kongo, they continued on burning plantations and killing 25 whites before being captured and beheaded. Their severed heads were mounted on stakes along major roadways to serve as a warning for others who might consider similar insurrections. Thirty-five to fifty Blacks were also killed.

Conspiracies and uprisings continued throughout slavery despite laws and tightened controls over enslaved populations. Aside from Nat Turner, and the Stono rebellion, Gabriel Prosser and Denmark Vesey and many others whose names are lost in history also led revolts, and hundreds of insurrections occurred on slave ships, most notably the Amistad with its leader Cinque, which occurred in 1839.

News of rebellions was quickly suppressed so as not to incite further insurrections. Curiously, during slavery, men on plantations were generally depicted as faithfully working in the fields; heads bowed and voices muted in obedience.

****

Although not as fragile and emotionally raw as we were over a century and a half ago when our ancestors embarked upon an uncertain journey to freedom, residual *nigger* wounds still exist among African Americans. Rap and hip hop culture have undoubtedly anesthetized our sensibilities, but their vacuous, over the top usage has no political or healing power and is out of sync with their "people give words power", philosophy. Gangsta nigga thug, bling, bling power is compromised fake power, trapped in misogynistic, ego-centered expressions and I *don't give a damn nigger language* which no one is bound to respect. If we don't give a damn, why should anyone else care?

What hasn't been considered is that outside of their rap, hip hop circles, *nigger* still has the power to get folk killed, and shows no signs of dying a natural death. The quality of their usage tells us what they think of themselves and reinforces long-held opinions of African Americans propensity for violence and criminal behaviors. In today's real world, our out of control niggas pose more of a threat to Black dignity and pride than the antebellum men and women who had little choice in what they answered to. Self-respect DOES count.

We must remember that the American white man's *nigger* was the invention of the master class, the white man, to whom they assigned questionable morals and character traits. However, our ancestors flipped the script and re-imagined the white man's nigger, creating a new conversation which became code for brother, blood, and friend. This communications strategy confused the ruling class and gave our ancestors a disguised and temporary sense of power. By reaching deep and connecting with their ancient Nega, our forebears were practicing Kugichagulia or Self-Determination long before Kwanzaa was created. Once we embrace Nega as a royal personification of nigger and nigga, we've won a critical round in

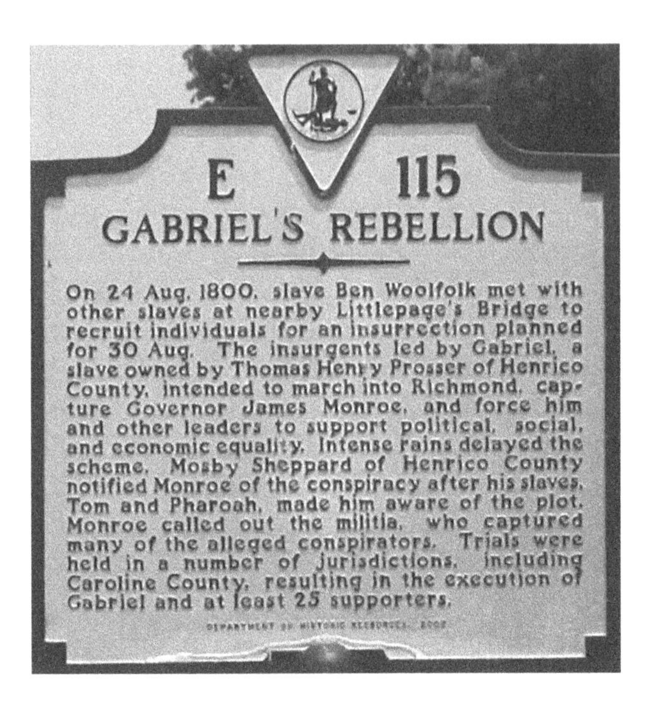

reclaiming the best and highest of ourselves. And what's so divine; we can still be Negas.

****

Greek philosopher, Heraclitus, is credited with saying "change is the only constant in life;" yet we know that change is not always welcomed or easy to accept. Change is a mystery; a venture into the unknown. Initially, we may think change is not good, only to find out it was the best thing that could have happened; and vice-versa. Or, we see both sides of change as we are experiencing it. For example; there was a time when white folks addressed Blacks disparagingly as nigger to their face without consequence. As we gained a sturdier footing, we raised our heads, fists, and voices and took a perilous step toward change. We began to fight back when assaulted. Many lives were lost defending their humanity against a powerful and compelling word.

The 1960's was a radical decade of change for all Americans, but there were three significant events which kick-started new directions for African Americans and the nation: The passing of the 1954 Brown versus Board of Education school desegregation law; the 1955 murder of 15 year old Emmett Till in Mississippi, and the 14-month Montgomery bus boycott which ended on December 20, 1956[18]. These events were a mixed bag of victories and outrage which gave Black Americans the courage to take their struggle for justice and human dignity to the next level of change.

On February 1, 1960, the country witnessed this bold insistence upon serious change when students in Greensboro, North Carolina staged a sit-in protest at a Woolworth's lunch counter that did not serve Black people. When these non-violent protesters refused to leave they were beaten and arrested, but the impact of their actions led to similar sit-ins throughout the south and changes in segregationist policies in Woolworth's and other businesses in the south. A replica of this lunch counter protest is an important installation at the Smithsonian's National Museum of African American History and Culture in Washington, DC.

The history of violence and injustice perpetrated by whites in the name of nigger had us perceive the word as a constant and persistent enemy of Black people. Even though Blacks had their

---

18 **a. Brown vs Board of Education,**Topeka, Kansas; 1954. Thurgood Marshall, the first African American to sit on the Supreme Court, led the fight that outlawed segregation in public schools.

b. Emmett Louis Till (July 25, 1941 - August 28, 1955) In 1955,15 year old Emmett Till from Chicago was brutally murdered and thrown into the Tallahatchie River in Mississippi after being accused of disrespecting a white woman in her family's grocery store.

c. Montgomery Bus Boycott: Rosa Parks was arrested for refusing to give up her seat to a white man resulting in the boycott which began in December,1955 lasting13 months. Boycott ended after the United States Supreme Court ruled that segregation on public buses was unconstitutional.

own intimate relationship with the word, whites held the power to emotionally unravel Blacks when it was used against them or in their presence. Whites continue to dictate how we internalize the word and hip-hop's polluted romance with nigga won't solve this dilemma. Claiming our Nega heritage and our unique culture are the weapons we need to use to bring about this change.

****

Black Power; Black is Beautiful; Back to Africa movements, and the passage of Civil Rights legislature in the 1960's provided a little relief when we were violated; but nigger was an ever-present provocateur. Only now, whites weren't as brazen and African Americans were not as passive. Whites did not use nigger negatively in the presence of Blacks unless specifically looking for trouble, while Blacks used the term the way they always have; mostly friendly, sometimes not. Public nigger referencing was not widespread and was usually confined to Black on Black dialogue in Black communities.

It's shameful enough that we are twenty-one years into a new century and the public and private abuse of nigga by Blacks has escalated to a nauseating crescendo. But it is just plain dumb and a breach of racial and family pride and protocol to permit others not invested in African Americans or the issues that concern us, to disrespect the sorrow and exploit the sacredness of our ancestors' perseverance and genius on their journey through American racism.

Rebuilding self-worth can begin with retiring Nigga from these mean streets to the private place where all other ethnic and family confidence matters reside. In this space, supported by cultural understanding and love, we will be able to seriously focus on our reimaging task. This is when Black power will become real enough to turn our strivings and struggles into a major triumph over nigger and nigga slave mentalities. Choosing not to do the work required to wear the crown could mean becoming a victim of legalized slavery, or just another nigga without a purpose or a dream. They're still around, falling off the radar every day.

Sadly, for self-proclaimed new niggas of all ethnicities on the streets without dreams and goals, not much is sacred. Whites who pretend to be niggas know their whiteness will always be affirmed. They may understand the rage and passion of Blacks who speak to pressing concerns and their awareness around these issues may have been raised, but wiggas do not carry the African American soul and spirit in their consciousness or historical memory which means we do not share common ground in this area which means they cannot be '*a homeboy, he ain't heavy, he's my brother nigga*'. Period!

****

In the early development of rap music, before *nigga, bitch, fuck, ho* became essential language for rappers seeking record deals, rappers were brilliant poets and wordsmiths who wrote meaningful lyrics about the sufferings and aspirations of Black people in America. Through their word artistry, they were able to crystallize the politics of white supremacy, government failures, and Black responsibility for attaining self-determination. Nigger was not off limits, but it was not violated and exploited. They used the term, as did the rappin' 'Last Poets' of the 1960's, when they told niggers time was running out; taunted them for being afraid of revolution, and charged them with 'waking up'. Many did open their eyes and saw who their real enemies were!

Spoken word artists, poets and rappers in the social and political tradition of Afrika Bambaataa and the Universal Zulu Nation followed in the 1970's. Gil Scott Heron's, "The Revolution Will Not Be Televised" taken from a slogan used during the Civil Rights and Black Power movements of the 1960's, became an anthem which laid the foundation for later rappers who spoke truth to power.

Rappers of this caliber did not become mega millionaires. Their reward was the raising of our social and political awareness which equated to human currency. They are the artists we will remember as un-bought, uncompromised, and the creators of an important music genre that spoke truth to power and raised the consciousness of generations who were hungry for knowledge of self and the system that conceals this knowledge. Gangsta nigga sellouts give us very little to celebrate.

****

Once hip-hop and gangsta rap culture became a hot, money-making commodity with marketing strategies for worldwide consumption, the game changed; and two, maybe three generations were exposed, some indoctrinated, into a sub-culture which defies decency. Their *mocking, cursing, threatening, distasteful rhyming* may make them popular among like-minds and they may rake in the cash, but they have not enhanced the art and soul of rap and hip hop or appealed to those of us who appreciate free expression, but respect messages of truth without denigrating those they profess to love.

Historically, Black music is a language which communicates love, joy, pain, and a range of emotions that go to the heart of our humanity. Our music has sustained us through hard times and still provides a refuge and healing space while we move through the ups and downs of daily living. Gangsta lyrics incite violence and disrespect. This is not what our forefathers envisioned and is not in the tradition of African Americans striving for equality, justice, love of self, family and community.

East/West gang nonsense and gangsta bravado in the rap game benefitted a few financially, and got more than a few killed in the prime of their lives. Elders always said, "if you live by the sword, you will die by the sword." Matthew; Chapter 26:52 of the Good Book put it this way, "for all those having taken *the* sword will perish by *the* sword." Unlike Cosa Nostra and Mafia gangsters who kill each other in far more brutal and dramatic ways than our gangsta bad boys, their code of honor emphasizes respect for culture, family and children.

Even though gangsta has lost some of its notoriety, it left a stain on our African American musical culture. The real time fallout is acted out every day by wayward youth with guns who more often kill other Blacks. Police are licensed to kill, and the gangsters within their ranks do so with impunity. In their eyes, these hip hop, go for bad, wanna be gangstas, encourage their being killed by making themselves killable; incriminated by lyrics of their gangsta rap role models.

Of special interest are rappers who profited from their talents and came to appreciate their success and are today making wise investments; becoming business and entrepreneurial role models giving back to their communities. Billionaire Shawn Corey Carter, aka J.Z.; millionaire Sean Combs, aka Puff Daddy or P. Diddy, and Curtis Jackson, better known as 50 Cent, come immediately to mind.

Richard Griffin aka Professor Griff of the 1980's political and militant rap group Public Enemy, is now a hip hop culture lecturer who teaches the *science* of hip hop. While Public Enemy was not part of the gangsta movement and their lyrics are known for speaking truth to power, I mention Professor Griff as an example of someone who comes out of a conscious rap IQ, taking the art form into the spiritual realm of understanding its importance and relevance to the African American struggle. Professor Griff shares his teachings with us on the YouTube channel and in lectures around the country.

It is clear to me that education, culture, spiritual strength, economic strength, and community, are essential for success in our strivings and struggles. Our ancestors survived due to their spiritual strength, and lifted themselves up with education, culture, and the support of family and community which enabled them to build strong economies and communities. These are the weapons we must have and use to wage war in this world where so little value is placed on Black lives. This is where we will find our own solutions to our problems.

****

Just as negative nigger ideologies were systematically put in place and believed by large segments of our society, the same can be done with positive Negus images and new ways of thinking about the old nigger. Reimaging and re-imagining should not erase the violence suffered in the name of nigger, instead, it will symbolize our escape from the clutches of mental slavery. We must first own our history before we can do what needs to be done to deal with the traumatic aspects of our experiences.

When we seriously consider the Nigus/Negus/Nega Ethiopian connection as a strong and plausible tie to our esteemed history, we will have an intelligent way of internalizing and interacting with this still potent word. Just as our ancestors made a way out of no way, we too, can do anything we make up our minds to do! We are a people who make magic when we IMAGINE, CREATE, AND ACT!

****

People of color are already a global majority and within the next few decades, will outnumber whites in the United States of America. People who classify themselves as white are not too happy about this nor it is a time for people of color to celebrate. During the coming years leading up to this demographic shift, we need to prepare our future leaders for leadership in what we trust will be a changed world where new directions in community building, education, and our rightful place in the world will be in process or already established.

By that time our sons and daughters will be home reflecting and thinking critically about the bygone gangsta era and understanding why African Americans are thought to be undeserving and why low expectations for our children's success have been normalized. Free of gangsta and prison mentalities, our now mature and reformed Negus will express their 'them against the world' anger in ways that will affirm and promote the best of Black humanity and culture. This is how pain will be turned into power!

6. WHAT YOU CALL ME OR WHAT I ANSWER TO?

"Nothing in the world is more dangerous than sincere ignorance and conscientious stupidity"

Dr. Martin Luther King, Jr.

By the beginning of the twentieth century, the term *colored* was used interchangeably with Negro as polite references for African American men, women, and children. Nigra was semi-polite for women, while Nigress was used to reference young women and girls. The impolite form of address for all African Americans, especially males, was... you guessed it, *niggers.*

The Black Power movement of the 1960's ushered in the *Afro-American* phase, with *Negro* holding its own among Blacks who were set in their ways, or not yet ready to publicly unite with their African heritage. By the 1980's, African American became the politically correct reference, particularly popular with white people; while Black people use African American and Black interchangeably. Negro is just about phased out, used mostly to reproach African Americans of little courage and because primary users of the term have joined, or will soon join, the ancestors. African, Nubian and Pan-African are also popular in particular communities.

Throughout centuries of changing identity labels, what is indisputable is that *nigger* has remained a steady descriptive and thrives today in a multi-cultural global environment. Its spelling has been changed, and perhaps its intention within rap and hip hop communities; however, for everybody else, it's pretty much business as usual. Whites continue to use nigger as an assault weapon; Blacks continue to use it in friendly fashion, while a segment of whites and Blacks have substituted the "N" word because of the dreadful side of nigger history.

****

In cities and towns around the country, nigga usage has become normalized. Users say it's not the same and point to its different spelling and usage in this new day of so-called diversity. But for me and many others who think like me, everyday sensibilities far outweigh any positive results we haven't yet seen since nigga supposedly changed its meaning making it free for all to use without discretion.

When our forefathers and mothers were enslaved and later lived with Jim Crow, Black Codes, shootings and lynchings, they may have answered to *nigger*, but a strong, silent racial integrity did not sway them from their goals or from the standards they set which the next four to five generations held close.

****

Nurtured in our social, educational, and political life, *nigger*, adjective or noun, is woven throughout the American narrative. Even when spoken out of habit by poor, ignorant white people, without seeming malice, the underlying implication is, *I am better than you.*

My parents told stories of the indignities they experienced growing up in small South and North Carolina country towns under strict Jim Crow Laws where nigger, lazy nigger, black nigger, nigger boy, ole nigger and any other adjective was used to describe and reference hard-working Black men, fathers, grandfathers, brothers, and uncles whose voices were muted. We were told that poor whites, commonly called 'white trash' were often the meanest and most hateful offenders. I believe that back then, as it is today, being able to utter the word nigger (nigga) makes white supremacy real for them. I will add that if and when whites were referenced as niggers, the understanding was they were niggers because they were poor and ignorant. But still forgivably white!

I remember my mother lowering her voice when she told us *"you know white folk don't talk much about their trash."* To her point, I have never heard whites speak disdainfully about poor, ignorant whites or reference them as trash. They are more prone to refer to them as victims of class disparities, yet still entitled to rights and privileges compromised or denied Black people in this nation. How curious is it that a people who claim to be superior expend so much time, energy, and money attacking Black humanity and repressing their progress. Just sayin' !

****

I first heard the term *American* African at a planning meeting of educators when an elderly gentleman commented on our being referenced as African Americans. He explained that *American* African is more appropriate for us and should also be the model for Africans born in the Dispora. He went on to say that African

American has African as the adjective describing the noun or proper name, American. This tells us what kind of Americans we are; whereas American African reverses the adjective/noun and tells us what kind of *Africans* we are and connects us more forcefully to the African continent. Afro-Cuban, Afro Puerto Rican, Afro-Brazilian, fall under the same pattern as African American, except Afro is not a country. Cuban African, Puerto Rican African, Brazilian African would be the proper references using this model. We needn't take short cuts or use abbreviations when we speak of our heritage.

There is no denying our actual places of birth. If born in the United States, we are by law American. We are simply shifting words around to make a statement about our proper ancestral heritage and identity. We claim the entire African continent as our roots spread wide and deep into cultures that are diverse and steeped in traditions and spiritual wisdom.

****

Unlike our forebears who accepted various labels without making a fuss, today we can choose how we wish to be referenced as a group and as individuals, and we can ignore those who call us out of our name. Nigger is not the culprit when used with discretion by Blacks among Blacks who have long had their own understanding of the term. However, in this curious and bizarre all-inclusive landscape, nigga may be friendly in the hip-hop, rap world, but the nigga, bitch, ho language; the ridiculous nigga style of saggin which often accompanies abusive nigger talk, and the mentality that going to jail is an honorable accomplishment is far removed from the hard-working, ole school Negus who tipped their hat with a "good morning, darling; have a nice day", when a lady walked by. We know and love these beautiful, strong Negus who respect themselves, family and community. While the world of hip hop and rap may see their language and behavior as free expression, I see it as an illusion of free expression that keeps them in bondage.

There are certainly communities of high-achieving and respectful hip-hoppers who answer to nigga, yet the proliferation of niggas with guns, gangstas on world stages, and saggin' hoppers in the streets, suggests standards have been lowered and we live in fear in our own communities.

We know the underpinnings of our White Supremacy/Racist system had its hand in orchestrating today's gangsta nigga climate that leads to early deaths and mass incarceration of African American males. Yet, behaviors which do not honor ourselves is a reality we must hold ourselves accountable for; remembering always that non-Black niggas receive a different kind of justice.

The moral here is, it's not what we are called; it's what we answer to. When we respond to versions of nigger; bitch/ho and any other reference that dishonors our character and values, we may as well tell the world, we have no character and values and that Black lives do not matter. So what do we do or say when they see us and kill us? Do you see the connection?

7. GRIOTS, DJ'S, NIGGAS, RAPPERS, AND GANGSTAS

"language influences thoughts and behaviors"

Storytelling is an ancient, universal form of entertaining, educating, and passing on important aspects of culture and traditions. In West African societies, storytelling is woven into the social, educational, artistic and spiritual lives of children. Stories and folktales are passed down by elders to instill the ethics, morals, and values of their family, tribe and community as well as teach young people the art of listening.

Anyone who could read and hold the attention of a child or larger audience could be a story teller. Then there are the Master Storytellers who are poets, musicians, performers and historians who travel within local villages and towns recounting and interpreting significant events in the lives of the people. These praise singers and keepers of legends and family lineages are known as Griots (Gree-oh) and various other titles in West African and Central African nations.

Griots are traditionally males born into Griot families and trained by their fathers in the art of storytelling, recitations of family histories, proverbs and philosophy; all very important in the life of the village. Guardians of ancestral legacies and oral traditions, Griots have the ability to present their stories so that even the very young listen and learn. An indigenous stringed instrument similar to a guitar or violin known as a kora often accompanies their presentation and *performance.* In essence, Griots are African rappers who interpret life events and entertain as do rappers in America. The difference is obviously in the message.

As a frequent traveler to Africa, my interactions with young children are reminiscent of my own youth when there was respect, good manners, and no thought of the kind of behavior on constant display in many communities around America. We weren't angels, but age appropriate behavior was a must in the company of others, especially our elders. Talking back to our parents, if we dared, had consequences that weren't good. Music of the day talked about love, respect, good times, and sometimes reinforced responsibility in our home and community life.

For example, an all time favorite of my 1950's generation was a song entitled *Yakety Yak* sung by a group called the Coasters. Listen up gangsta nigga rappers, and followers. This song was a huge hit, becoming the #1R&B (Rhythm and Blues) song on the Billboard Chart in 1958. *Yakety Yak* is a forever song. Here is a sampling

Take out the papers and the trash
Or you don't get no spendin' cash
If you don't scrub that kitchen floor
You ain't gonna rock and roll no more
Yakety yak (don't talk back)

Just finish cleanin' up your room
Let's see that dust fly with that broom
Get all that garbage out of sight
Or you don't go out Friday night
Yakety yak (Don't talk back)

How's this for back in the day music reinforcing messages of responsibility for maintaining our homes and minding our manners. Thanks to technology, Yakety Yak sung by the original Coasters can be seen on the You Tube.com channel. Please listen. I guarantee you will enjoy!

Then there was *Earth Angel*, a classic *do-wop* love song which was a huge hit in 1955 and can still make us feel warm and fuzzy. Ladies were angels on earth, not bitches and ho's on the corner. And we ladies loved it!

Earth angel, earth angel, will you be mine?
my darling dear, love you all the time
I'm just a fool, a fool in love with you
Earth angel, earth angel, the one I adore
love you forever and ever more
I'm just a fool.a fool in love with you
I fell for you and I knew, the vision of your love-loveliness
I hope and I pray that someday.
I'll be the vision of your hap-happiness oh, oh, oh, oh!.

Corny? Perhaps! But love songs always
made us smile and feel good.

****

Some of the best music on the planet was produced by Motown Records in the motor city, or town of Detroit, Michigan. Motown nourished us throughout the turbulent 1960's and 70's and continues as a mainstay in American music, heard as backdrop in movies, commercials, special events, and is classic listening in many parts of the world.

Gangstas have Death Row Records, Lowlife, Mo Thugs, and Konvict Muzik Records and the music they produced reflects their thoughts and lifestyles. Unfortunately, respectable language and behavior is not what it used to be. Thoughts have changed the language; language has changed the behaviors, and technology has made the world smaller and easier to influence.

****

Contrary to what some folk believe, Africans did not lose their culture when brought forcibly to the new world. They simply did what metaphysicians do; they reinvented themselves, merging the old with the new to create their own distinct ways of expressing themselves. Throughout the Americas and the Caribbean, most notably Haiti, Brazil and Cuba, new religious and social systems were created borrowing from old traditions which survived the journey. To practice their forbidden spiritual traditions, they merged them with religious and social systems imposed upon them by their Catholic colonizers; France, Portugal, and Spain.

African spirit and nature gods honored in Haitian Voudou, Brazilian Condomble, and Cuban Santeria rituals and ceremonies, express themselves through Saints of the Catholic faith. For example, when paying homage to St. Peter, they were also calling on Elegba, guardian of the Crossroads. This syncretizing of Elega with St. Peter is fitting as St. Peter holds the keys to the gates of heaven, while Elegba opens the road and allows passage between the material and spiritual worlds. There are variations in syncretizing African deities with Catholic saints, but the ideology is the same; saints are stand-ins for traditional deities. Versions of organized African spiritual systems and individual supernatural, magico beliefs are practiced today in every corner of the world.

Our ancestors also brought their drums, chants and rhythms giving birth to America's greatest music. Spirituals or sorrow songs born out of the sufferings of enslavement; field hollers, call and response work songs to help pass the cotton-picking days in the fields and labor-intensive chain gangs. Gospel music, praise songs of faith and the goodness of God; blues, telling stories of love gone wrong and making it through hard times; ragtime, jazz, scat singing, bebop, rhythm and blues, and rap, all originating from the Black experience in America.

Rap music has impacted the world and has certainly earned its place in musical history; yet only time will tell if the gangsta brand of this music will be acknowledged as a worthwhile contribution to our musical legacy. I will only concede gangsta's worth if held up as an example of WHAT NOT to honor in the musical legacy Black people have given the world.

****

In the 1950's and 60's radio market, Douglas "Jocko" Henderson was one of the first Black disc jockeys in Baltimore, Philadelphia, and New York who always opened his "Rocketship" show with an out of space introduction and his trademark rap before *taking off* into his musical stratosphere:

"Eee-tiddly-ock.
This is the jock.
And I'm back on the scene with the record machine,
saying ooh-pop-a-doo, how do you do. . .?
This is your ace... from outer space...
not the duplicator... not the imitator... not the impersonator...
but the originator!"

Jocko was an early forerunner of today's rap culture and brought his unique brand of rapping and spinning rhythm and blues discs to Black radio audiences who grooved and rapped right along with him.

Black disc jockeys have always done more than spin vinyl. They provided information important to the lives of their listeners and their communities. Foul and unbecoming language of any sort was off limits and never once did I hear mention of nigger, bitch, or ho over the airwaves. Black radio was a family affair. There was no concern that elders and children would hear the kind of foul language we hear today. We performed chores to music, paused to do a two-step, and prayed our favorite song was going to be the next tune up.

Disc jockeys had to be as good as the music they played in order to develop and maintain loyal followers. This meant knowing their listeners, creating their own style of communicating and knowing what music to spin. Community happenings and entertaining dialogue were also important.

One of the all-time greats in the tradition of rapping disc jockeys, most notably in the New York market, was the Chief Rocker and radio programming innovator, Frankie Crocker who played the music we most wanted to hear from the 1970's up until shortly before his death in 2000. Crocker was smooth, arrogant, and influenced many disc jockeys of his day. He informed us that "if Frankie Crocker isn't on your radio, then your radio isn't really on"; and his promise to "put a glide in our stride and a dip in our hip" made him a beloved favorite with fans. Never any cussing or nigger talk; just Black love, and the honoring of his promise to put that dip in our hips and that glide in our stride.

There were other radio jockeys who established close relationships with their audiences, and through the music and their personal commentaries, shared positive stories and affirmations, humor, community news, shout-outs and the always beloved 'special dedications'.

****

In back-in-the-day Black communities, teens and young adults engaged in a form of street games and entertainment played out among friends on the block, referred to in some neighborhoods as street joshing, snapping, and several other names which were essentially soft insults slinging back and forth between players. The object was to get the best of the opponent by drawing the heartiest laughs from bystanders. *Sounding* and *playing the dozens* were two of the most popular battle of wits between two *game*-players, usually male, who were brave enough to withstand being ridiculed and laughed at.

Sounding usually started when someone was called out for doing or saying something stupid. The response was an insulting retaliation followed by additional slamming and shaming banter. Mostly harmless word play made up on the spot, sounding was an oral performance which could attack any aspect of a person's being with the hope of drawing a laugh, or a *snap* in the language of Black slang. The unofficial winner was the one who persevered and made onlookers laugh out loud.

Sounding sometimes caused hurt feelings and could go way down hill if a line was crossed and the *sound* cut too deep. For example, sounding about mental or physical handicaps, illegitimacy matters, and other hurtful truths which caused personal and family embarrassment, could end in a fight and fracture once upon a time happy friendships. Injured participants usually recovered and friendships mended, but they rarely got back in the game with the same opponent unless their verbal and mental skills had improved.

Playing the dozens followed the same format, except insults targeted mothers, fathers and family members; but mostly mothers. Fat, stupid, ugly and poor were the basic words used in the attacks which were mostly funny but not always harmless. For example; "your mama's so FAT, after she got off the carousel, the horse limped for a week." Or, "Yo momma's so fat, when God said, "Let there be light," he asked your mother to move out of the way." If the opponent's mother was really overweight and the laughter loud, the situation could get out of hand but never violent.

As language went from benign, playful insults, players began to incorporate sexual conquests involving one's mother or other family members. This version of the dozens was delivered in a rhyming mode. Still funny but tough skin was necessary to endure these kinds of attacks on your mother. Here's an example:

I fucked your mama, till she went blind,
Her breath smells bad, but she sure can grind.

I fucked your mama for a solid hour,
Baby came out, screaming, Black Power!

Of course, this was all supposed to be humorous and a platform for exhibiting African American verbal dexterity. Only those who knew how to frame language and create rhymes and poetry on the spot were successful at playing the dozens and survive being demoralized. Once a rhyme was used, it had to be retired and new ones created spontaneously. It was not a game for sissies.

Playing the dozens is said to go back to slavery times. Ossie Guffy recounts in her 1971 *Autobiography of a Black Woman*, her grandfather's lecture: He told her that "the slaves played the dozens but that it wasn't for fun. They were playing to teach themselves and their sons how to stay alive. The whole idea was to learn to take whatever the master said to you without answering back or hitting him 'cause that was the way a slave had to be, so he could go on living. It maybe was a bad game, but it was necessary. It ain't necessary now."

Richard Majors and Janet Mancini Billson, write in their book, *Cool Pose: The Dilemmas of Black Manhood in America,* that "playing the dozens prepares Black men "for socio- economic problems they may later face and facilitates their search for masculinity, pride, status, social competence and expressive sexuality." Whether we agree with this analogy or not, there is little doubt that the toughening up that comes from playing the dozens could be a good thing for Black men to have when facing demoralizing hostilities.

The African version of Griot *rappin'* had shifted from important and entertaining cultural and history lessons for the villagers, to a rap insult fest for on the block observers whose role was to instigate further put-downs. However, even in times when the laughter stopped and tempers flared, *nigger* was not a term used in their ire. You were more likely to hear, "I'm gonna kick your ass, boy! Or, "I don't play that shit, faggot". In the 1950's and 60's, we knew and used cuss words out of the hearing of elders, but nigger was not a word on our personal radar. That has all changed. Playing the dozens has moved off the block and is now played on stages all around the world where gangsta rappers perform and denigrate women.

****

Researching beginnings, it is generally accepted that present day rap began in The Bronx, New York when a DJ was experimenting with his turntable at his sister's back to school party in the summer of 1973. He scratched and extended instrumental dance beats and rapped in between breaks. Rapping became a part of the DJ's repertoire and they began hiring themselves out for parties and other community and social events. Spinning vinyl recordings on two turntables, cutting tunes in and out interspersed with poetry and rhymes that moved the crowd to the dance floor, and kept the people happy and the party going, became the craze. The skill of the DJ's rapping and the music they innovated on their turntables determined the success of the party. Break-dancing or the intricate body-moves seen danced on the streets was sometimes added for extra entertainment and crowd pleasure.

Rapping and hip hop was growing and having its social and political impact on artists within the Zulu Nation headed by Afrika Bambaataa, but rap had not yet blown up, nor was this so-called *new* art form taken seriously by the music industry early on. This changed in 1979 when three young brothers from New York City who called themselves The Sugar Hill Gang, released a single entitled Rapper's Delight. Recognized as the song which kick-started mainstream hip hop in the United States and abroad, Rapper's Delight was the first commercially successful rap recording. Playful and catchy lyrics to a hip hop tempo showcased personal possessions, physical attributes, and a dance beat everyone could move to. In 2011, Rolling Stone magazine ranked Rappers Delight #251 of their 500 Greatest Songs of All Time.

The phenomenon caught on and went from rappers honing their *skillz* at house and block parties, and other community events, to a worldwide movement that has influenced the way young people and us older folk too, think and interpret the entertainment, political, social and racial environments we now inhabit.

****

Grandmaster Flash and the Furious Five broke new ground in 1982 with their social and political hit, "The Message", the first rap recording that spoke to the never-ending trials and tribulations of life in Black ghettos around the nation. The refrain:

"Don't push me, cause I'm close to the edge,
I'm tryin' not to lose my head.
It's like a jungle sometimes
It makes me wonder how I keep from going under"

became the anthem for disenfranchised young men who felt trapped in their go-no-where circumstances. "The Message" told it like it was and could have been interpreted as a warning. Things could get scary if too many Black men were pushed over the edge.

"The Message" is acknowledged as the first rap song to reflect stinging realities of Black life in the ghetto and the stress of living with...

'Rats in the front room, roaches in the back
Junkies in the alley with the baseball bat
I tried to get away but I couldn't get far
Cause a man with a tow truck repossessed my car"

"The Message" was delivered without nigga, bitch, or ho language, but the passage of time brought little relief from the conditions people live with and suffer through. As police brutality and other systemic frustrations continued the language and behaviors of rap and hip hop culture changed to reflect their pessimism with the system. Abrasive and graphic lyrics glorifying gun violence, anti-police rhetoric, and kinky sex moved in.

****

Rap music that actually had intelligent and righteous messages which spoke to the inequities African Americans faced was never aggressively promoted to mass crossover audiences, while the evolution of Gangsta was furthered and fully embraced by corporate pimps who made offers gangsta rappers could not refuse. The opportunity to exploit this new, unconscious music was in their face. To get the big record deals, all rappers had to do was spew out violence and self-denigrating lyrics at home and abroad; let the world hear and see their disregard for the sacrifices of their ancestors and talk bad about their women. Let the world see what they'll do for money.

The aphorism that money is the root of all evil is not correct. The Bible says, "for the *love* of money, is the root of all evil." (I Timothy 6:10) This must be true because what else could or would have our talented young wordsmiths abandon themes of "power to the people; we want freedom, in favor of "I'm rollin' with my niggas Dre and Eastwood, Fuckin' hoes, clockin' dough, up to no good"; and "I got nuts to bust, and butts to fuck, and ups to shut, and sluts to fucking uppercut," not to mention the despicable, "rape a pregnant bitch and tell my friends I had a threesome". Lordhamercy! Where did we go wrong? [19]

Rap songs such as N.W.A's (Niggaz With Attitudes) Fuck Tha Police, stupidly and unnecessarily suggests that, "Punk police are afraid of me! HUH, a young nigga on the warpath; And when I'm finished, it's gonna be a bloodbath of cops, dying in L.A." Yo, Dre, I got something to say. Fuck tha police! Fuck tha police" and Ice-T's "Cop Killer" with lyrics that ask, "what you're gonna be when you grown up? Cop killer, good choice, I'm a muthafuckin' cop killer." [20]

These are angry and frightening responses to police brutality across the country. Mainstream Blacks generally understand the anger yet have difficulty with how it is expressed. In reality; however, these imposter gangstas do not kill police, they kill each other. More importantly, if the objective of rappers who use this kind of language is to die at the hands of the police, they're on the right track. Otherwise, wisdom and propriety dictates that even if we think in the language of 'fuck tha police', there is nothing to be gained by verbalizing these sentiments for the world to hear. Feel good rhetoric can be foolish when we consider that police forces around the country have their share of gangstas, who by the way as we all know are licensed to carry guns and kill. Nevertheless, it is these kinds of lyrics which gained mass appeal among our youth and wanna be hood gangstas and created riches for corporate

---

19 "I'm rollin' with my niggas Dre and Eastwood, Fuckin' hoes, clockin' dough, up to no good" Dr. Dre; Snoop Dogg, "Bitches Ain't Shit" album; 1992
"I got nuts to bust, and butts to fuck, and ups to shut, and sluts to fucking uppercut." Earl by Earl Sweatshirt, 2011
"rape a pregnant bitch and tell my friends I had a threesome." Tron Cat from Album Goblin; Tyler, the Creator, 2011

20 Fuck Tha Police; NWA (Niggaz with Attitudes) Album Straight Outta Compton, 1988

producers and a few gangsta artists, some of whom passed on before they could fully enjoy their ill-gotten gains.

****

Blinded by the bling, gangsta rappers welcomed the money changers into their street temples and made deals that would reduce their mothers, sisters, aunts, daughters, wives, lovers and friends to vulgar sound bites in worldwide media markets. Sadly, when low-life rap and gangsta hip hop lifestyles have played out and whites and other non-Black niggas grow up, pull-up, and join the establishment, we know who will be left holding the bag of shame.

There is little nourishment or comfort in music that glorifies guns and drugs. These are the niggas who can be maimed, killed, and left for dead in an alley by one of their own or the police. These are the niggas who really don't get that they are creating a destructive blueprint for their own demise.

8. THE "N" WORD: MERRIAM WEBSTER, HUCK FINN AND WHITE NIGGA RIGHTS

"To know what lies ahead, listen to those coming back"

To whitewash the term nigger and try to mentally remove it from its racially infested root, African American *never-users* and *politically correct* whites have bonded with the "N" word, an inauthentic, less threatening euphemism that can be verbalized with more civility. The "N" word eases the discomfort of whites who say they *share our pain;* Blacks who wish to *rid themselves of the pain*, and removes the perceived offensiveness of the word itself out of the way; however, it does not offer a different paradigm for interpretation. This passivity and non-descript substitute has reduced this powerful word to a hollow sound bite. I do not accept this. Nigger is too important in our history to be reduced in this manner.

When I hear the N word, I may as well hear nigger. The N word personifies the lie we keep telling and changes nothing except pronunciation. A white progressive colleague once told me, "I just can't say, you know, the "N" word", meaning nigger. I asked why as saying the "N' word only changed the sound of the utterance, not its meaning and imagery in the minds of hearers. Response: "I just can't say it". My initial thought was, "wow"; a disguised expression of white supremacy. Here's why!

I agree that nobody, including Blacks, should *ever* speak the word nigger irreverently. However, "N" word users have given inauthentic communication a higher priority than truth. It's their way of renouncing the ugliness of white nigger usage, without changing the images that come to mind when we think about nigger. White progressives and liberals love the "N" word which provides more access to the word without offending sensibilities, theirs and ours. Their justification is that "N" word usage is out of respect for African Americans. I find this interesting in that when used authentically and in right circumstances, there is no disrespect. It's truth. When used without malice and in the proper context such as education, relating an incident where nigger was used, or diversity trainings, the more authentic it's use, the more effective the training.

Let's face it, Blacks and whites have been acculturated in the same racist American society which means that white progressives and liberals are not exempt from pre-conceived nigger notions. This is foolish for whites to deny, and for Blacks to think otherwise. So we may as well keep it real, make it plain, and come to grips with the good, the bad, and the ugly surrounding nigger and its impact in our lives.

Blacks who use the "N" word do so for a different reason. For them, nigger carries a long history of pain and aggravated assault on Black humanity they would rather not be reminded of. For them the white man's nigger is the only nigger there is, even though nigger has lived happily in the Black world side by side with whites. Perhaps, this writing, particularly the chapter entitled, Toms, Coons, Mulattos and Mammies will provide a different perspective on the part nigger played in keeping us sane. Our strength and resilience lie in our historical past of which nigger figures prominently. Therefore, nigger usage in the proper context maintains the truth of the word without altering its history, as nigga and the N word have the possibility of doing.

According to an independently produced documentary entitled "The Four Horseman" which can be viewed on the You Tube channel, we have entered the age of consequences where issues such as climate change, migration, conflicts, national security and global stability are being seriously impacted by past abuses and misdeeds. I would add slavery, race, and atrocities committed in the name of nigger to this list of consequences yet to be faced and karmic debts yet to be reckoned with.

If we are to release ourselves from mental slavery, we must embrace and revere our ancestors slave experience; their struggles through Jim Crow; constant nigger threats to their dignity; celebrate their triumphs, and honor the rich legacies left us to build upon to insure continuing progress of the race. Hopefully, the day will come when we stop hiding from this history; even call it out and promote it from the perspective of who built what white folks enjoy; who laid the foundation for their wealth? We do not have to reinvent the wheel. We can learn from our Jewish brothers and sisters who insist they will 'never again' suffer the atrocities experienced under Adolph Hitler and his Mein Kampf ideology. Never again!

To avoid our past and carry anger like a ton of bricks weighing us down, is to discount the sacrifices made on our behalf which enables us to choose the road on which we walk, however rough and crooked it may be. Just as our enslaved fathers and mothers were builders, we can follow in their footsteps and also build. We have much to resurrect and reclaim.

****

"N" word brothers and sisters exist under the same white supremacy code and are victimized the same as niggers everywhere. So, what is the *real* reason for this silly substitute besides acknowledging that white usage still wields the ultimate power; a power I trust will be reversed once Black folk have a fuller, historical reference for who the real Negus are.

What I see in this "N" word sham and multi-ethnic nigga is the laying of the foundation for the eventual rewriting of nigger history. I believe in the not too distant future, the offensive and abusive history of the word will be gradually redefined to reflect yet another lie. The terror nigger once held for African Americans exclusively will be buried deep in the historical record, recasting the offenders as our best friends forever as perpetrated by rap, hip-hop, and urban culture who bought into the lie. History books will represent niggas as inclusive of Americans of all ethnicities, each having equal access to the American dream.

Rewriting slave history entirely may present a challenge, but over time, this too can be whitewashed to present a less harsh reality. Tampering with historical facts has been done before and fake news is not new. Rather than apologize for slavery and offer up reparations to begin healing the trauma our entire country suffers, seems our government would rather play the *not guilty; it didn't happen like that* card. By now we should know, the ruling population in America ain't got no shame; and having a conscience is open for debate. We better make our case before a manipulated historical record invalidates any claim African Americans make for reparations. It's already been thirty-two years since a bill to study reparations was introduced in Congress in 1989 and every year since.

****

For the first time in more than ten years, a House Judiciary subcommittee held hearings on June 19th, 2019 to discuss reparations for descendants of those enslaved in this country. By the time this committee meets again, and another hearing held, and results examined and re-submitted to yet another judicial body, the lawmakers involved will be long gone and the process will start all over again. You all know how this works! However, momentum is growing and the call for reparations has been energized with some movement towards this goal taking place on local levels rather than the federal government.

The City Council of Asheville, a small town in North Carolina has voted to pay reparations "for its participation in and sanctioning of the enslavement of Black people". California has agreed to establish a task force to study how reparations could be implemented, and a few local governments are doing the same. This makes me wonder if the United States government has the spine to reckon with its true history. Seems the moral fiber required to apologize for her sins against Black humanity and atone by paying reparations simply isn't there.

****

One of our master teachers, Dr. John Henrik Clarke, told us a long ago, "we have no friends". And we've heard the old adage, "if we don't learn from the past, we are doomed to repeat it". The new Jim Crow and the modern-day colonization of Africa is an example of both these aphorisms.

Dr. Clarke also reminds us that "history is a clock that people use to tell their political and cultural time of day... history tells a people where they have been; what they have been; where they are and what they are. Most important, history tells a people where they still must go, what they still must be." As descendants of the oldest people on the planet, we have been everywhere, and have occupied thrones and seats of authority. Where we are and what we are today varies, but the crucial questions are where we still must go, and once again become. This means we must have a vision for the future and pass the baton to our next generation who must be prepared to take our struggles and strivings to the next summit.

Universal, multi-racial nigga makes no worthy contribution to the map of where we must go and does not model who we still must be. We ourselves can choose the history we write and the legacy we leave, but we have to do the work.

Once the work is done and nigger, the "N" word, and nigga becomes Negus or Nega in word, deed, and conscious mentality, progressives and liberals will be in the predicament of having to use Negus and think 'of high status' instead of low-life thug, something whites will likely not do. Not sure how they will deal with this dilemma but I suspect nigga use as we know it will come to an abrupt end.

****

Under pressure from the National Association for the Advancement of Colored People, Merriam Webster's Collegiate Dictionary agreed to delete the negative association of *nigger* with Black people, now defining it as:

- "expressive of racial hatred and bigotry; and
- its use by and among Blacks is not always intended or taken as offensive."

Internet dictionaries, slang dictionaries, and updated standard dictionaries, give varying definitions which go from "an extremely offensive word in reference to Black people", to "African Americans using nigger 'self-referentially' among themselves"; to "the Irish are the niggers of Europe".

****

Mark Twain's American classic, *Adventures of Huckleberry Finn,* was banned from the Concord Library in Massachusetts shortly after its publication in 1884 and has since been taken off the shelves and banned from school libraries around the country because the word *nigger* is used throughout the book over two hundred times.

Amid charges of censorship, New South Books published a sanitized edition of Tom Sawyer and Huck Finn, taking nigger out of the book entirely, replacing it with the word *slave* in some passages.

On June 12, 2011, 60 Minutes (CBS) aired a segment on the *cleaned-up* version of Huckleberry Finn, and a refreshing interview with professor David Bradley of Oregon State University who 'loves' the word nigger, and says he asks his class to say the word out loud eight times before they begin to analyze Huck Finn. "How can a nation come to terms with nigger if it's not discussed openly and honestly?" Bradley understands the historical reality of nigger, yet appreciates the word from his own Black perspective. This episode is still available on You Tube and is worth viewing. https://youtu.be/nW9-qee1m9o

****

Among Black people, *nigger* is a metaphor for comrade, extended family, homeboy, fellow victim, survivor, and an inner knowing of who the antagonists are. Even those who do not use the term understand the way it is used and understood among Blacks. I have no doubt that even the most prominent, successful, uppity African American families have their nigger in the woodpile who may irk the hell out of everyone, but who is loved and welcomed just the same as long as the hard-core gangsta element is not part of his persona.

Removing nigger from Huckleberry Finn, the N word, and co-opting whites and others into Niggerdom has not, does not, and will not dispel long held opinions of Blacks being undeserving of anything that looks like equality and justice, prosperity and pride. This is what makes their acceptance into Niggerdom all the more objectionable. Were they told by white corporate creators of the gangsta brand that their own kind had to be a part of this rap, hip hop nigga movement or all bets are off? Or, is low self esteem and a need for white approval and acceptance the reason they allowed others to place their spirits on the altar?

No version of nigger should be used in friendly fashion with those whose ancestors used it to terrorize our people. I don't hear or remember hearing friendly use of chink, wop, spic, guinea, mick, or any other slur between diverse groups. Doesn't it seem odd that the most offensive insult of all has gone global? Nothing has been gained and nothing has changed by this show of generosity. In fact, it has gotten worse.

****

Controversy swirled around the term nigger in corporate media in June, 2007. Tom Burlington, a white Fox network news anchor in Philadelphia was fired for using the word nigga in the presence of African Americans. Burlington's lawsuit charges discrimination in that two of his Black colleagues used the term freely without being penalized. A United States district judge believed he made a valid argument. For the first time in history, a federal jury was asked to decide whether it is acceptable for African Americans, but not whites, to use the word in the workplace, referencing the Civil Rights Act of 1964, Title VII, which prohibits discrimination based on race, color, religion, sex, and national origin as the basis for the suit. This opened up new legal avenues that may prevent Black victims from taking legal action if the term is indiscriminately used in corporate America by non-Blacks if Blacks themselves use it among themselves in the company of whites and other ethnic groups.

Judge R. Barclay Surrick said, "When viewed in its historical context, one can see how people in general, and African Americans in particular, might react differently when a white person uses the word than if an African American uses it. Nevertheless, we are unable to conclude that this is a justifiable reason for permitting the Station to draw race-based distinctions between employees."

After numerous postponements, in 2015 an all-white federal jury unanimously handed up a verdict which rejected allegations of discrimination by Tom Burlington. Burlington was actually fired because his colleagues, most of whom were Black, refused to work with him.

After reading this account, it is easy for African Americans to say how wrong it was for Burlington to use the word in the workplace; yet according to the law, it is possible to conclude that he had every right to use the word since his Black colleagues used it freely. Does this amount to a double standard? Should there be a double standard? Or, is this a much needed wake-up call for undiscerning and myopic Black folk who violate nigger rule #1; keep nigger in the family. What we should absolutely know is that white folk do not want Black folk to have anything they cannot have. But who would have thought the day would come when they would want to take our nigga.

****

Over a four month period I conducted an informal, two-question survey among fifty African American participants; 35 male, 15 female. The eldest was an energetic 86; youngest 25, with representation from ages 30's, 40', 50's, and 60's. All live in urban areas on the east coast and are high school or college educated, middle class, non-problematic, US citizens who vote and hold jobs in government and corporations. Six are teachers and three social workers. No rappers or hip-hoppers. I wanted to know who in this group of American born Black people use or never use the word nigger and why; and should white people and other ethnicities be allowed to use the term freely in everyday conversation in the company of Black people?

The results were not surprising. There were twenty-two "never users" because of its abusive use by whites throughout our history; (b) twenty-eight "*friendly*" users, not abusers, within the family, comrade model, with all fifty participants rejecting use across racial lines, including within hip-hop communities.

The *never users* consisted of eighteen females and four males, who happened to be the oldest participants; the youngest 48. Each held unhappy memories around the word, clearly internalizing it from a white power perspective, yet acknowledging friendly use among Blacks. The four men acknowledged they used the term during their younger years, but stopped after joining the church, getting older, and not being around people who use the word. The twenty-eight *friendly users*; twenty males and eight females, use the term when it fits a situation, but only in the company of other Blacks. Nigger was not a part of their everyday conversations.

Not a scientific sampling, but enough to suggest that there is still sensitivity around white on Black use outside of rap and hip-hop communities where whites can reference Blacks as niggas without penalty. Rappers and hip hoppers may think this is outdated thinking, but I challenge them to analyze their own thoughts and why they think it's okay given what is happening in the country around issues of racial justice and equality. Whatever your point of view – respect yourself!

9. NIGGAS IN AFRICA: REVISITING THE TRADE

"The only real mistake is one from which we learn nothing"

The first time I heard the word nigger in Africa was in September, 2012. I arrived in the West African nation of Ghana two days before and was on the grounds of the Elmina Castle/Dungeons where captured Africans were imprisoned while waiting for ships that would take them across the Atlantic Ocean into enslavement. Now a Museum and World Heritage Site, thousands of tourists, scholars, educators, researchers, family re-union groups, and a growing number of Ghanaians pass through the main gate every year.

Each time I visit Ghana, I look forward to making my pilgrimage to the dungeons; to pass through the *door of return* to visit with ancestors and give thanks for their sacrifices and endurance. I especially remember the brave captives who jumped into dangerous waters trying to return home to Africa and perished while escaping a foreboding fate.

Moving towards the main entrance gate, I ran into a Ghanaian woman I've known over the years who sells cloth and souvenir items on the dungeon grounds. While exchanging greetings and updates, the usual groups of young men who also sell souvenirs and local art work, besieged a group of tourists disembarking from a bus anxiously urging them to 'take a look; take a look' and guiding them towards their goods spread out on the ground. Two young men did stop as others kept walking towards the entrance to the dungeons assuring the vendors they would stop and look when they finished their tour.

I was about to say good-bye and continue on to the dungeons when we heard one of the young men yell out rather loudly, "twenty dollars for this cheap junk" as he and his friend began to walk away laughing. Their nuance and tone indicated they were insulted by what seemed a rip-off price. One of the Africans responded with a crotch gesture and a brash "American niggas" at which he and his fellow entrepreneurs also laughed. I was stunned. In my forty years of travel to various countries on the African continent, this was a first. I looked at Adjoa in disbelief. It occurred to me this may have gone another way had these young tourists known something about the African bargaining system.

****

As I stood in disbelief, Adjoa began to share her thoughts on the changing youth scene in Ghana and the influence American movies, television, videos and music being aired on Ghanaian radio and television is having on young people. She went on to say how a growing number of young Ghanaian men use bad language and smoke marijuana and we both agreed that for them, these are cool American behaviors. Since nigger holds no history for them, nigga means rap, hip-hop, twerking, money and a way of living they can only wish for.

Not only do many Ghanaians not know the whole truth about nigger, most of the *castle* entrepreneurs have little knowledge of what took place behind those dungeon walls or the history and struggles of Black people in America. Those who know a little, consider the ones taken away lucky and privileged, with money to give away. Our young peddlers may have thought they would receive a different kind of interest or possibly a sale. But all they got was a laugh that said '*these Africans are crazy*'. In actuality, they are not crazy. They are surviving. The riches of their country still overwhelmingly benefit former European colonizers, newcomer Asians, and corrupt politicians.

It's disheartening to think that the promise of the first sub-Saharan nation to gain independence from Britain in 1957 led by Dr. Kwame Nkrumah, father of Pan Africanism would fall victim to another round of mind control. *Nigga-rizing* Africans, and making drugs available and then criminalizing its victims are the latest psychological and material strategies being used to confuse and ultimately dominate the people; the same tactics used to destabilize communities of color all over America and the world.

****

Ghanaian anthropologist, Dr. Datey Kumodzie has looked long and hard at what he terms, Africa's *socio-economic tragedy*; particularly in sub-Saharan Africa. Here is some of what his research revealed:

"Africa's early contact with foreign cultures and lifestyles led her people to discard or suppress their own indigenous cultural heritage and knowledge foundation in favor of foreign languages, religions, philosophies, and symbolisms. This paradigm shift alienated Africans against their own culture; not understanding that adopted foreign cultures cannot, and will not solve their problems and move them forward."[21] This thinking has filtered down to newer generations and offers some insight as to why, with all of the gold and rich natural resources, Africa has not been able to reclaim herself from colonial domination, even in their independent status.

****

21 Africa, Why Are You Poor? Dr. Datey Kumodzie; Humanu Grafiks, Ghana 2009

When I shared my dungeon experience with my African American community who have made Ghana their permanent home, little surprise was expressed. They reminded me of my *'go - come'* status and affirmed the conversation I had with Adjoa. Things are changing. The influence of Western values and African American rap and hip-hop culture is more evident than ever. I must admit that in recent years I had noticed the growing preference for second hand European and American clothing and styles. Pants inching down and skirts inching waaaay up defy traditional African dress codes.

I have also read news stories of a changing Ghana, but I had never heard the word *nigga* come from an African's mouth; young or old. And then I realized, 'why not nigga?' That's the word streaming out of kiosk music shops where nigga infused hip-hop has replaced the traditional high life music that made you want to dance down the main street and into the market. Elder Africans seem oblivious. I suspect it is because they have accepted a changing world.

Early colonizers imposed language, education models, religions, and foreign values on their victims, but indigenous religious and cultural traditions managed to co-exist under the radar or in disguise. This time around, the seeds of cultural annihilation are being sown in African soil. This time, nigga has a prominent place at the *kill African culture* table.

****

Prior to the 1960's, the average African American also experienced a severe identity crisis, embracing everything European and despising their African origins, color and culture. The doll experiment first conducted in 1939 by psychologists Kenneth and Mamie Clark in New York City, showed us just how early Black children begin to internalize not being good enough and develop damaging feelings of inferiority.

When asked to choose the bad doll, Black children chose the Black doll; when asked which one was the pretty doll, they often chose the white one or none at all. Caribbean Blacks and continental Africans also prefer whiteness and snuggle up to them, but being the majority population in their countries and seeing their own in positions of authority help them to better maintain a measure of pride in their culture.

****

The Civil Rights and Black Power movements of the late 1950's and 60's, and the creation of Kwanzaa in 1966, our very own African American week-long holiday, saw many Negroes and Coloreds learning about and embracing their African roots and culture. Natural hairstyles became the signature statement of Black Pride, and wigs and skin lighteners moved on to African cities across the continent. Straight hair wigs and bad hair weaves are fashionable in Africa today, competing with a slow return to natural hair. Many of our continental sisters are coming back to their roots, proudly wearing their hair natural. In Ghana, thanks to the influence of African American sisters who visit and live in Ghana and wear their hair in locks, I now see locks adorning many former wig wearing, weaved, and chemically straightened heads. As their locks grow long and beautiful, they see that Black beauty cannot and should not be measured against white standards.

10. THE NEW BLACK

"The new Black is not new"

The "New Black" is a relatively recent descriptive given a bit of notoriety by Grammy-winning producer and songwriter Pharrell Williams during an April, 2014 interview with Oprah when he said, "the New Black doesn't blame other races for our issues. The New Black dreams and realizes that it's not pigmentation it's a mentality. And it's either going to work for you, or it's going to work against you. And you've got to pick the side you're gonna be on." [22]

There is truth in this reasoning, especially for those blessed with talents that afford privileged viewpoints and choices. They have 'made it' and are able to enjoy aspects of life made possible by their commitment and hard work; ***and*** lest we forget, by the sacrifices of our forebears who often kept their ego tightly shut up while putting their lives on the line to open doors *New Blacks* are able to walk through .

---

22 There are many accounts of this interview on the You Tube channel and print media that can be accessed via Google.

New Blacks do not deny racism exists, they simply choose not to make race the reason for not achieving their goals. This is not a new ideology and in truth, race is not always a reason for not succeeding. We know there have always been prosperous African Americans who kept their heads down and took a distant public view of inequality and injustice, even during the Jim Crow era. They went about their business, making money, living above the poverty curve, educating their children, and enjoying middle to upper class lifestyles. They understood the 'ruling class' view of African Americans and chose to assimilate quietly into the American mainstream.

Those who could pass for white crossed over, never to go back, but always looking over their shoulder for people like me who know the truth at first glance. I worked with a woman who passed herself off as Italian. She could have been an olive-toned Sicilian but her voice inflection, generous lips, and chemically straightened hair betrayed her. She spoke with a Brooklyn *Italian* accent, but I never heard her actually speak Italian.

****

African Americans who are living the American Dream, eat in fine restaurants, travel the world, and who interact with others who live similar lifestyles tend to think like Pharrell. There are also African Americans who live more modest middle class lives impacted by institutionalized racism, yet have no patience with chronic claims of victimization by Black people who haven't done as well. They may even be critical of them and blame their wayward lifestyles for their failures. However, these same people will mentor and open doors for young achievers who work hard and benefit from their role model and mentor relationships.

The generation born in the 1970's and 80's who think of themselves as belonging to this New Black and millennial culture are also the entitled generation. They did not experience the

1960's, the turbulent, angry decade that shocked the nation into paying attention to serious grievances such as systemic injustice and continuous racial inequality. Yet they are beneficiaries of the bold and courageous civil rights leaders, activists, and students who sat-in, marched, went to jail and died challenging this nation for the very things New Black millennials take for granted. The actions of these fearless men and women brought about change and legal protections for some of our grievances. For them, race was indeed a reason for being stopped at the front door.

****

Rapper/actor Common also acknowledges the existence of racism in America, but he has his own prescription for bringing it to an end. On Comedy Central's Daily Show back in March, 2015 he laid out his plan to host Jon Stewart. Here's what he said, "Hey, we all know there's been some bad history in our country. We know that racism exists. I'm extending a hand like, 'Hey, we want to get past this. We've been bullied, we've been beat down, but we don't want it anymore,'" said the rapper. "We're not extending a fist; we're not saying, you did us wrong!' It's more like, Hey, I'm extending my hand in love. Let's forget about the past as much as we can, and let's move from where we are now. How can we help each other?" This can still be viewed on YouTube. *Behind the Media 3-19-15 Common sense....sort of. Jon Stewart*

Sounds to me like Common has it all mixed up. Asking African Americans to forget about the past, which has to include slavery, is like asking Jews to forget about the Holocaust. Does he understand that the ruling class would love nothing better than for us to forget since they cannot find it within their hearts to say a sincere, "We're sorry we did you wrong and beat you down." And while we're extending our hand in love, Black bodies are being riddled with deadly bullets by police and community vigilantes, with justice and equality as elusive as ever. Besides, who forgets about their past?

Need I say it again, our resilience, creativity, spiritual and cultural distinctions are rooted in our past.

I try not to judge how people think of themselves and who they are being in the world. However, I know the truth of nigger wake up calls, even when successful, living righteously, and extending hands of love. If we don't receive *the call*, it means we are very good at being invisible or ignoring the ringing telephone.

****

Speaking of nigger wake up calls, Oprah had one some years ago in a very high-end boutique in Zurich, Switzerland. We all know Ms. Winfrey is a billionaire, yet when she asked to see a bag which cost $38,000, she reportedly was told that the bag was too expensive and was offered others of lesser value. This incident became a media event.

Six months before Oprah's call, Oscar winning actor, Forrest Whittaker was stopped and frisked when leaving a Manhattan West Side deli. We may also recall the 2009 arrest of distinguished Harvard Professor Dr. Henry Louis Gates, Jr., who was restrained in his own home after police were called by a neighbor who suspected he was a burglar. Even after showing his Harvard ID with his address, he was handcuffed, arrested, and treated disrespectfully for being 'unruly'.

No one is exempt from the call, no matter how educated or successful. Malcolm X posed the question long time ago, "What do you call a Black man with a Ph.D? Yup! You got it! *Nigger!*

****

New Blacks can choose to forget the past, play down race and racism, and believe their achievements are due solely to their own self-determination, hard work, and how they think. It's nice they think this way, but I hope they are mindful that their call could come at any time and any place, without warning.

I am hopeful this New Black, millennial generation, many who have national and international platforms, will appreciate who made it possible for them to do what they do and raise their own racially and politically conscious voices to push the ball forward. Joining the call for reparations for the centuries of free labor forced upon our ancestors is a good place to start. There is still much work to be done.

On another note, in the world of fashion if the new color for the season is projected to be the hottest new trend, it is referred to as the *new black* since the color black is always in vogue. Some use the phrase to mean *cool,* or to call out a baaad current style.

****

New *Niggas* arrived on the block in the mid to late 1980's all dressed up in new nigga *outfits* around the same time a segment of rap music began rapping about hard-core illusions of grandeur and manhood. This *gangsta* element of rappers defined the harsh realities of their lives with tough and nasty language, advocating, sex, drugs, violence and death. They rap truths that have the ruling class preparing their warfare strategies just in case, while rap and hip-hop devotees, captivated by the inflammatory, anti-establishment rhetoric to beats that have them bobbing and weaving, are throwing their hands up in the air - as if they didn't have a care.

Corporate media capitalists, usually white men whose priority is green supremacy in a white supremacy industry, saw the possibilities of gangsta rap and the opportunity to make MONEY! Lots of it! Their business sense told them this rap/hip-hop thing could easily be exploited. Creative teams were put together to observe and research Black urban culture and marketing strategies were developed which I believe are largely responsible for legitimizing *nigga* use and all of the other objectionable language used in gangta rap. Their research told them that the offer of record deals and the possibility of making more money than they could count would not be turned down. They were right! For these business tycoons who have little or no regard for Black people, *it's strictly business.*

Whites have played an enormous role in popularizing gangsta. As hefty consumers of rap music, they bring the worst of already stereotypical beliefs and behaviors into their personal space creating an intimacy with niggas which supports what they and their parents already believe; Black men are gansgtas and prone to violence. Plus, non-Blacks hear Black rappers, hip-hoppers, and urban youth using the term nigga liberally, and decide it is okay for them to use it also. They, too, think the changed spelling makes it alright. Or, do they really? Our young brothers and sisters forget to remember that White Supremacy/ Racism are always in the room.

****

I reject friendly interracial use of the term nigga and believe Black on Black use should always be friendly and used with discernment, respect and in the spirit of Nega. Blacks who use the term need to know its history beginning with royal Ethiopian Negas; to rebellious negas on slave ships; plantation niggers who sabotaged their masters, and white American constructed nigger which includes nigga. Think brothers and sisters, whites and other non-Blacks are on a wild nigga joyride and can jump off whenever they feel like it.

There was a time when nigger talk was not publicly boisterous. If a nigger slipped out of a Black mouth in a public space, white and Black people would get uneasy and look away. Not so today! Nigga has been neutralized and it's all taken in stride because its meaning has supposedly changed, yet I see no evidence of change in the treatment of niggers. Believe what you see people!

****

New nigga rappers received record deals by compromising standards and boundaries. These *nouveau riche* Negroes, now able to indulge themselves with luxuries they've never known, have no idea of the responsibility that comes with life in the fast lane. They live large and spend generously on clothes, cars, jewelry, and their groupies who stay until the money runs out. The more astute rappers have become new Nega businessmen making wise investments and developing entrepreneurial enterprises accumulating wealth and reaching back to help their communities.

JZ and Puff Daddy both came out of came out of public housing and stay connected to their fans and, no doubt, ole school niggers who may have served as role models for them given their humble beginnings in Brooklyn and Harlem, New York. There are others who got woke and recreated their lives in the world of business. I hope they come to fully embrace the Negus/Nega image and use their celebrity and business status to promote this ideology. Why not come out with a line of redesigned, Black influenced crowns, t-shirts, and other merchandise inscribed with NEGA and NEGIST for males and females, children and adults. Subtle messages do infiltrate and change minds.

All niggas have a place in the royal palace; even gangstas. The only requirement is that they emerge from their dark tunnels ready to re-think who they are being in the world; and to think about what they're thinking and doing, and then question its intelligence. This requires a serious inner dialogue, when if examined properly and in the right spirit, should result in language which communicates love of our people and making it to higher ground together. This is when niggas, gangstas included, will finally be emancipated and brought home after a frightening and dangerous street life in the ghettos, alleyways, jails, corporate board rooms, and hip-hop/rap stages of the world. Come on home my brothers and sisters. Our time has arrived! Let's use it wisely.

****

The violence and terror nigger has triggered and the sorrow and despair suffered by families who lost loved ones as a result of *nigger incidents*, should never be erased from our memory; nor should we write nigger out of our national narrative. Nigger is as much a part of America as her original African captives and American born offspring and this history is vital to understanding how we arrived where we are and to serve as a reminder of where we need to go as a nation.

Today's nigga epidemic is being exploited to the detriment of Black people. The gansgta nigga mentality has contributed to a culture of constant reminders that *Black lives don't matter*; even their own. Only when we return to our original teachings and gain control of our African mind, will we be able to renew ourselves and transform the hearts and minds of our people.

If gangstas appreciated the expanse of our history from the Nile Valley civilizations of Egypt and Sudan; great kingdoms and empires like Ethiopia, Cush, Ghana, Mali, Great Zimbabwe all of which flourished before colonial invasions; as well as our African American forefathers whose slave labor helped build America's wealth, they would have to concede they can do better. We have an inheritance that deserves to be honored with pride. This is how we add value to our lives, our history, and our legacy. This is what gives credence to Black Lives Matter.

11. LIGHTEN UP! LAUGHTER HEALS

"White gal ridin' in an airplane, yella gal ridin' the train
Black girl ridin' on a mule's ass, but she ridin' jes the same"

The African American experience in America is akin to Sisyphus of Greek mythology who was condemned for all eternity to rolling a large stone to the top of a hill, only to have it roll back down again, or trying to push cascading water uphill. Beginning with the first African captives brought to these shores, there has been little rest for the weary and we must always understand two worlds within one nation, and two words when only one has been uttered. Our elders called it 'reading between the lines'.

Black people have long been the last hired and first fired. We must work harder and be better while making less money and being overlooked for deserved promotions. African Americans endure insults, injustice, and attacks on our humanity, and are expected to keep quiet and often do. But our resilience, creative survival skills, and abiding faith in the righteousness of our cause, are direct benefits of these systemic inequalities.

However; what really makes us special and the envy of our detractors who can't figure out why we're still here, is our ability to laugh out loud. In my family, and families like mine everywhere, when we go through tough times, we invoke the word of God, cook comfort food, put on the music, and let the dancing and laughter begin. I doubt our forefathers and mothers could have come through the trials of their daily lives were it not for their innate ability to place crying on hold for a while, and create ways to have a good laugh and keep hope alive.

****

The average African American home did not own a television until the late 1940's, early 50's. During that time, television entertainment was family friendly variety shows featuring stand-up comedians, magicians, circus acts, ventriloquists, performing artists, and any other clean and friendly entertainment. Situation comedies, cowboy shows, detective dramas with little violence, and news broadcasts, all starring, with few exceptions, white people in white situations.

Seeing Black people on television in the 1950's and 60's was not common and when they were cast, it was usually in roles which reinforced Black lives in subservient and lowly situations. African American scientists, scholars, educators, or any Black person who had managed to achieve against all odds, were not highlighted. But we were so hungry to see people who looked like us, we watched and laughed anyway.

****

The face of comedy has changed since the mid-nineteenth century minstrel shows, where whites and Blacks performed in *blackface* imitating stereotypical characters and plantation life in the south. Vaudeville and burlesque were other forms of live entertainment where language was risqué but clean, clever, and made audiences laugh. A limited pool of Black comedy actors appeared in Hollywood movies and television in the 1930's, 40's and 50's.

Mantan Moreland gained popularity in Hollywood movies in the 30's and 40's. When he fell to the stereotypical depiction of the wide-eyed, nervous character in Charlie Chan films of the 1940's, he lost his appeal as Black people became more conscious about not supporting these kinds of representations.

Jack Benny was a white comedian who did vaudeville, radio, and had his own television series in the 1950's and 60's. Eddie 'Rochester' Anderson who played Benny's Black house butler was able to draw laughs without compromising his dignity and was often looked to for advice from his Boss Man.

Amos 'n Andy was one of my family's favorite television shows and enjoyed by lots of Black families around the country, whether they publicly admitted it or not. The main cast of characters included George 'Kingfish' Stevens; his wife Sapphire; Mama, Sapphire's mother; attorney Algonquin J. Calhoun; Andy Brown; Amos Jones; and Lightnin. I was fascinated with their names, especially Kingfish and Lightnin' because they were perfect metaphors for the characters they played and were easily recognized as part of the larger human family, as was each cast member.

Kingfish, properly dressed in white shirt, bow tie, and tail-type jacket was always cooking up a scheme which Andy, his humble and naive Lodge brother and sidekick would trustingly fall for. Amos was a hard working taxi driver and the voice of reason; Calhoun, the pontificating lawyer, while Lightnin' was the slow moving, slow talking janitor at their Lodge, The Mystic Knights of the Sea of which Kingfish was president. Sapphire and Mama wore stylish dresses, church hats, and enjoyed social activities.

Amos 'n Andy was good comedy delivered by seasoned Black actors who were working at a time when little work was available to them. A good part of the laughs was the Kingfish/mother-in-law encounters having to do with an idea the Kingfish had cooked up which she had little confidence in. By the end of the half-hour episodes, all was happily resolved.

Set in Harlem with an all Black cast of respectable characters living everyday lives in nice apartments who did not cuss or use the term nigger. Amos n' Andy was good clean fun and represented a slice of Black life we could relate to, but were not ready to see played out before the country during the 1950's Jim Crow era.

The irony is that the Jackie Gleason and the Honeymooners show, which made its television debut in 1955 and still enjoys re-runs and marathon airings, showcased similar characters living in a working class Brooklyn neighborhood. Ralph was a bus driver and his buddy Norton, worked in the sewers. Both were members of the Racoon Lodge. Ralph and his mother-in-law were always at each other's throat and Ralph was always cooking up a scheme which Norton usually fell for. Wives Alice and Trixie were best friends and housewives. The situations and dialogue in the Honeymooners were always funny. Even when I know the entire episodes by heart, the timeless dialogue still makes me laugh. Add Black nuance to this and you have Amos 'n Andy.

****

Amos 'n Andy began as a radio program created in 1928 by two white men impersonating Black characters. The Black cast of the television series first aired in 1951 and was immediately picketed by the NAAPC for poor representation of African Americans. Production stopped in 1953 but the program remained in syndication until 1966. I understand the outcry of the day as we were far from ready to deal with Kingfish, Lightin', or Calhoun characters and we were certainly not yet able to *publicly* laugh at ourselves for portraying what we call unflattering stereotypes in the human family. If I had to name one character that may have been mildly embarrassing, it would have to be Lightnin'. (He was slow-moving and slow talking. Get it!!!) For a fuller history of the

Amos 'n Andy Show and the pro and con issues around its airing, please see note. [23]

****

If any Hollywood created character cast a disparaging cloud over Black people, it was the infamous Stepin' Fetchit played by Lincoln Theodore Monroe Andrew Perry. Stepin' was the classical stereotype of a slow-witted, sluggish, rambling talker who was incoherent much of the time. White folks found him funny; some Black people did too, but he didn't work for me or my family.

Reflecting on Stepin' as I write this book, I cannot recall in all my years having ever seen a real live human male, female, or child who fit the characterization of a Stepin' Fetchit. It's no wonder he enjoyed a lucrative Hollywood career acting a sho' nuff fool who fit nicely into the stupid, lazy, dim-witted, white American nigger box. He made money in Hollywood, but he could not compare to the fine acting and sophisticated humor Amos n' Andy gave us. There are

---

23 The NAACP's national office published a bulletin on August 15, 1951 entitled Why The Amos 'n' Andy TV Show Should Be Taken Off The Air:

> It tends to strengthen the conclusion among uninformed and prejudiced people that Negroes are inferior, lazy, dumb, and dishonest.
> Every character in this one and only TV show with an all Negro cast is either a clown or a crook.
> Negro doctors are shown as quacks and thieves.
> Negro lawyers are shown as slippery cowards, ignorant of their profession and without ethics
> Negro women are shown as cackling, screaming shrews, in big mouthed close-ups, using street slang, just short of vulgarity
> All Negroes are shown as dodging work of any kind
> Millions of white Americans see this Amos 'n' Andy picture of Negroes and think the entire race is the same.

https://abernathymagazine.com/reflections-on-black-image-in-amos-n..andy/
Anatomy of a Controversy; Amos 'n Andy 1983 – YouTube.com

a number of You Tube clips and movies with Stepin' as well as full episodes of Amos 'n Andy. See for yourself!

****

By the 1950's and 60's, live stand-up comedy and recordings were popular with Black audiences. Comedians Red Foxx, Moms Mabley, Nipsey Russell, Slappy White, LaWanda Page, among others were naughty and sexually suggestive. Sprinkled throughout their monologues were double-entendre sexual innuendo and a nigger here and there; but no bitch, ho, motherfucker, or constant nigger, cussing language; and their nigger was always in the spirit of brotherhood. They too, were funny and made us laugh out loud. You can also see them in action on the YouTube channel.

Bill Cosby, who started as a stand-up comedian in 1961, was a master at telling hilarious squeaky-clean, everyday stories of growing up Black in America under the watchful eyes and loving arms of parents and communities who instilled values and healthy disciplines. Never any nigger crutches needed for him to touch our funny bone; just a good, wholesome sense of humor.

The 1970's, 80's saw Richard Pryor and Paul Mooney make racially diverse audiences laugh out loud with their heavily *niggerized* dialogues, which gained momentum on the Black comedy circuit. Pryor had an epiphany in Africa in 1979 which caused him to regret using the word. He stopped and was still funny.

Mooney admitted to abusing the term after his outrage at white comedian Michael Richards' *nigger* outbursts in a Los Angeles comedy club in 2006 [24]. This incident led him to speak out against its use, although he expressed concern that by making the word taboo, its power might be increased. Mooney also questioned

24 Michael Richards' *nigger* outbursts in Los Angeles comedy club in 2006
http://www.tmz.com/2006/11/20/kramers-racist-tirade-caught-on-tape

whether eradicating the word would do anything to change the sentiments and opinions of those who use it?

Admittedly, Pryor and Mooney were very funny. I get the *nigger* nuance and enjoy a well-timed and delivered *nigger* in satirical and comedic circumstances, delivered by Black comedians. Pryor's nigger, Mooney's nigger, and the niggers I know, bear no resemblance to white perceptions of nigger. Flawed though he may be, my nigger sees through the Willie Lynch scheme and refuses to be broken; coming from a tradition of heroes and survivors who used their minds and wits to rebel against their oppression and comfort each other in a country where it is hard for them to catch a break. Nigger humor was an integral part of this survival history, long before science recognized laughter as a healing balm for the soul.

****

White folks never *really* know *authentic, grown up* niggers who are not defined by white American standards. They may know about *nigger toes* (Brazil nuts) but they don't understand the humor in *nigger please!* Or, *he my nigger even if he don't get no bigger;* or the admiration in, *he's a fine nigger; a cool nigger,* and the always, ever-present in all Black families, *that crazy nigger.* [25]

Real niggers are wizards, creating magic while juggling the contradictions of being Black men in America. James Baldwin said, *"to be Black and conscious in America is to live in a constant state of rage."* Authentic, grown up niggers turn their rage into success and rise to the top in business, government, and entrepreneurial enterprises. They raise families, take vacations, and serve as role models in their communities. This is when we experience the *Nega soul* of Black men which comes in many spiritual and rhythmic forms that can't be fully explained or imitated. We just know it

25 Nigger Toes: Brazil Nuts are South American edible seeds that come mostly from trees in Bolivia and Brazil

when we see it. Former President Barack Obama has it, and I *know* his adversarial colleagues envied his swagger, Harvard backed intellect and South Side of Chicago street smarts, and said so behind closed doors. *Uppity nigger*!

During an Obama health care hearing before the House of Representatives in 2009, Republican, Joe Wilson restrained himself when he yelled at the President, "you lie" a first in the history of the House. While he had enough restraint to stop before completing his charge, Black people automatically read between the lines. Obama did too. Yet, of the public criticisms Wilson received from whites for his blatant disrespect, none spoke directly to the red-neck, South Carolinian's racist intent. President Obama was unflappable. This is what it means to be a cool, dignified Nega with a superior sense of humor. We know the President and his wife had a good laugh at that one.

****

Revisiting childhood times spent in the south, I always remember the laughter of my elders when they spoke about events that weren't all that funny to me. I now know much of their laughter emanated from their deep insights into the sick minds and actions of white people. They used humor to ease the pain, reduce stress and cope with their lives. Maya Angelou put it this way, "In spite of everything that was done to me and my race, in spite of the adversity and the bitter moments, again we rise." Humor and laughter always help us to rise!

12. DIE NIGGER DIE! RISE, NEGUS, RISE!

"An elephant does not die of one broken bone"

In 1964, the same year the Civil Rights Act was signed by President Lyndon Johnson, comedian Dick Gregory published an autobiography entitled, *Nigger.* Introductory remarks remind us that our ancestral "Momma...*didn't die a slave for nothing... those of us who weren't destroyed got stronger, got calluses on our souls. And now we're ready to change a system, a system where a white man can destroy a Black man with a single word. Nigger! "When we're through Momma",* says Gregory, *"there won't be any niggers anymore."*

A trusting assumption encouraged by the promise of the 1960's when Blacks were becoming more conscious and embracing their African heritage and culture; acknowledging their beauty; holding their heads up with pride; raising their fists high with determination, and becoming bold in demanding civil and human rights as promised in the Declaration of Independence. And when Brother Malcolm told us *"we had a right to be on this earth, to be a human being, to be respected as a human being in this society"*; to be achieved *"by any means necessary"*; and James Brown declared. *"say it loud, I'm Black and I'm proud"*, African Americans were infused with renewed strength and commitment to change an oppressive government system . Even those who didn't publicly support Malcolm knew the truth of his words.

The 1960's was also an angry and ugly decade of hatred and civil unrest in the nation. Justice and equality for African Americans were at the center of our domestic war, while young Black men fighting in Vietnam to protect America's interests were being disproportionately killed or returning home traumatized and drug addicted to a government that did not see them as heroes.

In 1966, the Black Panther Party for Self-Defense was founded in Oakland, California. Their 10-point program called for equality in education, housing, employment, civil rights, health care, freedom for political prisoners, and an end to police brutality and murder of Black people. Called "the greatest threat to the internal security of the country" by FBI Director, J. Edgar Hoover, Black Panther chapters were infiltrated by Negro field operatives leading to their eventual demise, only to be resurrected as the New Black Panther Party in 1989. Kwanzaa was also created in 1966 by Dr. Maulana Karenga who sees culture as the unifying principle for Black love, unity, and the way back to our original African greatness.

In 1967, Muhammad Ali, a recent convert to Islam under the tutelage of Malcolm X refused induction into the military on religious and political grounds. He spoke out against this country's racism and railed that "he had no quarrel with the Viet Cong; that no Viet Cong ever called him a nigger". Ali was convicted by the US government, stripped of his boxing title, and became an instant hero for Black people who admired his courage; and a loathsome outcast for whites who vilified him as ungrateful and unpatriotic.

Ali's conviction was overturned in 1971, and he went on to become the champion once again and acknowledged as one of the most beloved and respected human beings in modern history. The Greatest! A prime example of how public opinion changes when we stand on principle for what we believe and live with honor.

The next year at the 1968 Olympic Games in Mexico City, John Carlos and Tommie Smith, gold and bronze medalists in track, staged a silent protest against racial injustice by lowering their heads and raising their black gloved fists in a Black Power salute from the victory stand. They were both expelled from Olympic village and sent home where they were welcomed as heroes by the Black community. This iconic moment in history is also memorialized in a life-size sculpture in the Smithsonian's National Museum of African American History and Culture in Washington, DC.

Continuing decades-long traditions of standing up against racial injustice, the most recent protest in sports began in 2016 by football quarterback Colin Kaepernick who refused to salute the American flag, taking a knee instead. He lost his job with the San Francisco 49er's for not compromising his first amendment right in the face of racism. I can imagine the nigger language being spewed from the mouths of football officials, fans, and everyday whites who believe our talented, highly paid athletes should be grateful, obey the rules, and keep their mouths shut. While the system Dick Gregory speaks of has not changed, African Americans have grown into yet another awareness of how corrupt the system is and the actions we need to take to move the fight for justice forward. Reimaging nigga is one of them.

After the killings of George Floyd, Ahmaud Arbery, Breonna Taylor, Rayshard Brooks, and Elijah McClain, which came to light almost a year after it occurred, NBA and NFL players and owners came out in support of Black Lives Matter with many taking a knee, locking arms, or staying in their dressing room until after the National Anthem has been sung. Not all fans support this shift and have been heard to boo players when they take the field. America won't stop. And neither will we.

****

By the end of the 1960's, Medgar Evers, President John F. Kennedy, Malcolm X (El Hajj Malik Shabazz), Attorney General Robert F. Kennedy, Rev. Dr. Martin Luther King, Jr., and numerous others in the Civil Rights movement, were assassinated and murdered. Mississippi was the most hateful state in the nation, while the city of Birmingham, Alabama was the most murderous. There were so many bombings in Birmingham during this period, it was penned *Bomingham,* most infamous for the September 15, 1963 church bombing that killed four little Sunday school girls. Our nation had reached another moral and spiritual low, and it seemed that the "*arc of the universe was not bending towards justice.*"

After President John F. Kennedy's assassination in November, 1963, Lyndon Johnson moved forward with Kennedy's national War on Poverty initiative which was supposed to address the "problem of persistent poverty in the United States", and I suppose, assume more responsibility for the plight of the poor. The Food Stamps Act, Voting Rights, Fair Housing, Medicare/Medicaid, Head Start, and other pieces of legislation designed to eliminate inequality and poverty became law in1965. That was close to sixty years ago. Yet many Americans still go to bed hungry, voting rights continue to be unlawfully manipulated, discrimination in education, housing, and health care persists, and for many a white American, niggers are still niggers who are unworthy and undeserving of life and liberty.

Near the close of this tumultuous decade H. Rap Brown, now Jamil Abdullah Al-Amin published his autobiography "Die Nigger Die". Brown, a Black Power revolutionary served as chairman of the Student Nonviolent Coordinating Committee (SNCC) and for a short period, Minister of Justice for the Black Panther Party. He was also on the FBI's most wanted list for a time.

Brown was not talking about niggers senselessly killing each other like we see too much of today, rather organizing to challenge the various systems which oppress African Americans. His title can be interpreted a number of ways; death to niggers who are afraid of revolutionary action in order to bring about the change we wish to see; or niggers must be ready to die to bring about the change we wish to see. Both are valid and necessary components of successful rebellions.

Die Nigger Die is a handbook of Black consciousness and revolutionary ideologies. Brown coined the phrase "violence is as American as cherry pie" and is known for his "Burn, Baby, Burn" rallying cry. The 1969 original version of Die Nigger Die was not available for a time after seven or so re-printings. It is available once again; it's message still relevant. Brown was accused of killing two policemen in 2000 for which he is serving a life sentence. He maintains his innocence.

****

The Black Power movement of the 60's laid the groundwork for the often-called post Civil Rights era of the 1970's; a period of unprecedented African American *visibility,* some say gains, which produced a round of 'firsts' for Blacks in many aspects of American life.

In 1970, corporate executive and former United States Deputy Secretary of State, Dr. Clifton Wharton, Jr. was appointed president of Michigan State University; the first African-American to head a predominately white university. Kenneth Gibson becomes the first African-American mayor of Newark, NJ; Essence and Black Enterprise magazines begin publishing; Playwright Charles Gordone became the first African American to win the Pulitzer Prize in Drama for his play, "No Place to Be Somebody".

During this decade, the Congressional Black Caucus is established in Washington D.C.; Johnson Products becomes the first African-American owned company to be listed on a major U.S. stock exchange; Leroy "Satchel" Paige, the first former Negro Baseball League player is inducted into the Baseball Hall of Fame; New York Congresswoman Shirley Chisolm becomes the first African-American to campaign for the Democratic presidential nomination and model Beverly Johnson appears on the cover of *Glamour Magazine*, the first African American woman to be featured by a major fashion magazine. Driven by political and activist pressure and Civil Rights laws, America placed a few crumbs on the table and cracked a few doors to let a few African Americans wiggle through.

These celebrated triumphs suggested African Americans were arriving; on our way to becoming full-fledged Americans. We should have known better. The country had to build our hopes high before new ways to stop our progress yet again were firmly in place. By the early1980's, the new strategy was ready to be implemented. Crack cocaine hit the streets, followed by the Prison Industrial Complex which they knew would be needed once addictions led to crime.

Black communities across the country infiltrated with this highly addictive substance, became crime infested war zones for hard-working, decent people within these neighborhoods and hastened death for the addicted. Many of our best and brightest got caught up in crack's crushing clutches and fell off the radar. The heroin epidemic of the 1950's and 60's was troubling, but crack was and is devastating.

Now that white Americans are hooked on methamphetamine and dying in unprecedented numbers of other illegal and prescription drug abuse, we're suffering through an opioid epidemic which is receiving a lot of attention and economic support for treatment. Black addicts were criminal and put in jail. Of course, Black folks knew it was just a matter of time before drugs would enslave the descendants of the enslavers. Karmic retribution may be delayed, but it stays on the books until the debt is paid. And still we will rise!

****

13. SELF-DETERMINING NEGAS

"It's about self-realization and claiming our power"

If we are to undo hundreds of years of body and mind control to become our own masters, the second principle of Kwanzaa, *Kugichagulia*, or Self-Determination - must be consistently practiced. Kwanzaa creator Dr. Maulana Karenga says that in order to be self-determining, we must "*define ourselves, name ourselves, create for ourselves, and speak for ourselves – instead of being defined, named, and spoken for by others*". African Americans know something about this principle which is also an excellent test case for applying Humpty's *who will be master* philosophy.

Nigger is not an enemy, it's a word! How this word is internalized and presented in the world is what this conversation is about. It's about gangsta nigga looking in the mirror. It's about reimagining, reinvention, reimaging, and ultimately, self-realization. When we know that words and actions do have the power to create and alter our personal and racial reality. It's about holding ourselves accountable.

Black people are not responsible for what is wrong in this country. We needn't blame ourselves and remain victims. It was our ancestors who were kidnapped, sold into slavery, and made to labor for hundreds of years without ever receiving a paycheck.

It was Black people who were attacked, harassed, lynched, denied, and suffered all manner of brutality at the hands of whites for no other reason than being of African descent and trying to uplift themselves. This was their payment for building the wealth of this nation. Unable to apologize for this breach in humanity, the system continues to justify slavery by turning African Americans into disposable liabilities.

Given this history and clear evidence of America's ethical and moral deficiencies, who among you would want to be defined by her standards? Our right to define ourselves was given to us by our Creator, and when we convince ourselves and act in our own behalf, we will no longer be an insignificant people in this country. We will claim ourselves; stop believing what others tell us to believe about ourselves, and push even harder to further change a system we may have thought could not be penetrated but whose walls are slowly falling down. When this happens, white America's greatest fears will be realized. We will come into the fullness of our political, social, intellectual and creative brilliance and there will be no stopping us from achieving what we always knew was possible.

****

Emancipation from slavery did not mean self-determining lives for the newly freed. Persistent racial harassments, the failure of Reconstruction, Ku Klux Klan terrorism, lynchings, Jim Crow, and every kind of provocation we can think of, made it clear white folk were not about to allow African Americans to enjoy their freedom.

As far as haters were concerned, Black people would remain suppressed and oppressed no matter what the Emancipation Proclamation or the Thirteenth Amendment said. It did not matter that African Americans overwhelmingly obeyed the law; believed in the promises of America and worked hard at becoming worthy in the eyes of the nation. The ruling class did not care about admirable qualities, nor were they interested in making amends or righting any wrongs. And the law was officially and unofficially on their side.

Facing continuous obstacles, our bold and resilient ancestor survivors on a mission made a way out of no way and left us with the grit that gave us the strength to continue our strivings. Were they looked upon and treated as niggers by the establishment? You bet they were. But they chose to rebel from within; with prayer; dreams, hope, committed actions and an ever-enduring belief they would be victorious. As they prayed and kept the faith, they built businesses, schools, churches, clubs, organizations, newspapers and founded towns that provided for the needs of its inhabitants. And they steadily prospered.

Our earliest scholars, educators, inventors, athletes, musicians, writers, entrepreneurs, activists and professionals were all contributors to this educated, upward bound New Negro class who had the will to succeed and set high standards for excellence.

Booker T. Washington, born into slavery in 1856, became the founder of Tuskegee Institute in 1881, known today as Tuskegee University, one of our most important historically Black colleges.

Scholar and activist, Dr. W.E.B. DuBois, born free in1868 became the first African American to earn a Ph.D. from Harvard University in 1895. One of his landmark books, "The Souls of Black Folk", is required reading in Black Studies classes in high schools and universities around the country. Dr. DuBois co-founded the NAACP and supported Pan-Africanism in word and deed. He was invited to the West African nation of Ghana by President Kwame Nkrumah to work on the Encyclopedia Africana. He died and is buried on the grounds of the W.E.B. DuBois Memorial Center for Pan African Culture in Ghana, next to the ashes of his activist wife Shirley Graham DuBois.

Dr. Carter G. Woodson, Father of Black History and founder of the Journal of Negro History in 1916, was born in 1875. He established Negro History Week in 1926, which became Black History Month in 1976. Dr. Woodson, whose parents bought their freedom, earned his Ph.D.in history from Harvard University in 1912. He wrote and co-authored numerous articles and books; most notably "The Mis-Education of the Negro" published in 1933. Still available and must reading for understanding how educational models in the United States do not serve Black students.

Marcus Garvey, born in Jamaica in 1887 where he founded the United Negro Improvement Association in 1912, settled in New York City and formed a chapter of the organization in Harlem in 1917. The UNIA became one of the largest Black Nationalist and Pan Africanist movements in the country, with global outreach.

Garvey's philosophy promoted social, political, and economic freedom for Blacks and called for a *Back to Africa* exodus from the United States. It is believed Malcolm X's father was a Garveyite and his death may be a result of his activism. Garvey's ideologies are respected and followed by supporters around the country.

African American women were also instrumental in freedom movements; community building as teachers, nurses, entrepreneurs, activists, and support for Black men in the struggle.

Imagine the courage it took for Harriet Tubman, birth name Araminta Ross to bring slaves out of bondage into freedom under the threat of death. And, for Isabella Baumfree to escape from slavery with her infant daughter, change her name to Sojourner Truth, and devote the rest of her life to speaking out against slavery and gender and racial inequalities. And, of course, Ida B. Wells, born in Mississippi in 1863, the year Abraham Lincoln signed the Emancipation Proclamation, who became a journalist and Civil Rights activist and led one of the early anti-lynching movements.

These heroes and sheroes represent a teeny, tiny fraction of Black scholars, scientists, activists, educators, clergy, judges, inventors, entertainers, artists, civil servants, and average hard-working citizens instrumental in the progress we have made with far fewer resources and support available today. These pioneers left footprints for us to step into as we continue to influence and shape America's collective consciousness. They were *real* Negus and Nigists of strong stock who managed the system of White Supremacy/Racism without disrespecting themselves, our ancestors, or our heritage. We remember them and we thank them.

****

By the early 20th century Blacks from the south began moving northeast, west, and Midwest to escape southern Jim Crow laws and seek better opportunities. Chicago, St. Louis, Cleveland, Los

Angeles, Detroit, New York, and other urban areas became new homes for thousands. In New York, an intellectual and artistic class would usher in one of the most important eras in Black literature and the arts; The Harlem Renaissance, which showcased music, theatre, literature, art and a growing political awareness. Harlem became the Black capital of the world.

White supremacy and racism was also active up north, but these *New Negroes* in Harlem wrote and created works that expressed the Black point of view without apology. Philosopher, Phi Beta Kappa, Rhodes Scholar, Alain Locke, (1886-1954) who studied at Oxford University; University of Berlin and received his Ph.D. from Harvard University in 1918, borrowed the phrase, *The New Negro*, for an anthology of essays, poetry, plays, short stories, art and music by writers of the Harlem Renaissance, and other interpreters of *Negro* culture. Locke became known as the father of the Harlem Renaissance which flourished during the 1920's; its contributors gaining worldwide attention. *The New Negro* collection, published in 1925 has been called the manifesto of the New Negro Movement. Locke became the head of the Department of Philosophy at Howard University, retiring after more than forty years.

One of our most beloved legacies of the Renaissance period is the 135th Street Harlem branch of the New York Public Library system, where the private collection of Arturo Alphonso Schomburg consisting of over ten thousand books, volumes, manuscripts, etchings, portraits, and pamphlets documenting Black culture were first housed.

Acquired by the Library in 1925, the collection was first known as The Negro Division. Shortly after Mr. Schomburg's death in 1938, the Division was renamed the Schomburg Collection of Negro Literature, History and Prints. In 1972, the Schomburg was designated a Research Library, one of four in the New York Public Library system, and was renamed the Schomburg Center for Research in Black Culture. Today, the collection houses more than eleven million testaments to the accomplishments and genius of Africa and her children in the Dispora and is one of the world's premier research libraries for African and African Dispora information and scholarship.

Before technology controlled our lives making access to information as easy as thumping our fingers on a keyboard, libraries, after school activities, social clubs, and the Black Church were our educational retreats. These venues of mental nourishment, cultural values, and spiritual guidance, reinforced positive home training and encouraged reading and learning in preparation for success in school and life in general.

Young people today are besieged with all kinds of media much of which are diversions from real life traumas they may be experiencing. Gangs, drugs, poor performing schools and students, and high unemployment among Black youth all contribute to deteriorating social skills and the inability to compete academically. Gangsta rap, nigga culture, and toxic aspects of hip hop culture figures prominently in this notable decline in the morals and values of those who believe these social aberrations validate their anger and excuse destructive behavior. If we are to reclaim our youth who are at risk of being legally enslaved in America, reimaging and reclaiming our noble African Nega is an absolute must!

****

The crash of the New York Stock Market in 1929 disrupted the movement and the Renaissance came to an unofficial end. The country sunk into the worst economic decline in modern history known as the Great Depression. Huge financial losses led to suicide and soup lines. To rebuild the country's economy and infrastructure President Franklin D. Roosevelt came up with his New Deal creating the Works Progress Administration 'back to work' program in 1935 which provided jobs for millions of Americans.

The Federal Art Project, an arm of the WPA, commissioned artists to paint murals in hospitals and other public institutions and established theatre companies, and writing projects. Slave Narratives from the Federal Writer's Project, is an important collection of more than 2,300 first person accounts of slavery. The Manuscripts, Prints, and Photographs Divisions of the *Library of Congress* preserved and edited transcripts and have made them electronically available to the public. These historical narratives and photographs live in the spirit and souls of Black folk, just as slavery reels around fearfully in the minds and conscience of white folk.

By 1938 the country was in recovery, followed by the start of World War II in 1941. African American men went to war in a segregated military as they did in every war, including the American Revolution to fight for freedom from colonizer Great Britain. African American women served as nurses and other non-battlefield positions, some making careers of their military service. Racism was always a factor; nevertheless, they committed to fight fascism and make the world a better and safer place for all. They also hoped their service would eradicate the inequalities and injustices they faced at home. However, upon returning home, our brave soldiers faced the same discrimination they have always had to fight against. Even when wearing their American military uniforms, they were still called niggers and spat upon by the same old cast of white bigots. Even so, Black folk just kept inching along like poor inch worms, making step by step inroads and recreating their reality to fit their circumstances.

****

When we consider that Black progress is always under attack, we have made extraordinary achievements. Nigger has beaten us down and strengthened our resolve to stand back up. Our particular circumstance in this country has taught the serious ones among us not to allow the psychological mindset of *victim* to render us helpless in our own cause for freedom and justice. There is no question African Americans have been victimized, but we do not have to remain victims. Victims are dependent, voiceless, powerless, and pitiful. Redefining the *nigger* white supremacy created as our African rooted royal Nega will change the name of the nigga game and the word that has come to represent Black people negatively, whether we like it or not. Redefining will raise self-esteem and empower our communities at home and abroad.

We can give our account of the hunt when we acknowledge that our Black American *nigger* has long been an ally who can make us laugh, cry, understand, misunderstand, hurt, love, and all manner of emotions that connect us to our humanity and shared history. As the process of changing the nigger/nigga paradigm to our ancient Nega model, anti-nigger attacks will continue to occur. Our responsibility is to stay focused and do our part to move us forward. Our forefathers and mothers, all of whom were undoubtedly called *niggers* and worse, knew who they were, what they stood for, and the goals they were determined to work towards. We must do the same and prepare the way for our next generation just as our ancestors did for us.

In the meanwhile, if we are to be niggers and niggas, let us be the best representatives we can be in our time on this planet. Remembering the anguish and accomplishments of our past, we strengthen our consciousness and come to know our heroes and sheroes more intimately. We are being thrown a lifeline back to our roots and original eminence. Grab it!

****

When we remember that Nat Turner rebelled because he and his fellow captives were tired of being enslaved; Frederick Douglass raised his voice against slavery because it was hypocritical to expressed American values; Ida B. Wells crusaded against lynching because it was inhumane; Dr. Carter G. Woodson researched and taught us our history so we could learn of our accomplishments; Booker T. Washington established an educational institution to enhance our skills and knowledge of the world and ourselves; Marcus Garvey organized the largest Black nationalist movement in the country to agitate for justice and a back to Africa movement; Arthur Schomburg collected our history and left proof of our genius; Thurgood Marshall defended our right to a quality education and helped desegregate schools; Paul Robeson sang and spoke out in support of human rights; Adam Clayton Powell, Jr. boldly used his legislative power to better all lives; Dr. Martin Luther King, Jr. and supporters of all races and faiths marched to change the world; and Malcolm X spoke truth to power, as did James Baldwin, Eartha Kitt, Nina Simone, Fannie Lou Hamer, Rosa Parks, and so many others. These heroes and sheroes are just a sampling of the many who stepped out and made significant contributions to Black strivings and struggles during a more dangerous time.

We remember those who were murdered. We remember the dogs, water hoses, billy clubs, rocks, vile words, church bombings, lynchings, draggings, emasculations, railroad track murders, KKK cross burnings, and all other tortuous behaviors perpetrated on a people unable to fully defend themselves. We remember these turbulent times by honoring the teachings and sacrifices of our elders and by respecting the sadness and the sacredness of the term that was synonymous with the terrorism they lived under. Get woke! Re-imagine, reimage and reclaim your crown.

14. PATHOLOGY OF THE WHITE IMAGINATION

"Privilege does not mean peace"

Historian, anthropologist, and Nobel Prize nominee, Michael Bradley, writes in his book, *The Iceman Inheritance; Prehistoric Sources of Western Man's Racism, Sexism and Aggression*, that "the problem with the world is white men" and "that racism is a predisposition of the white race".[26] Since no one alive today was present in prehistoric times, we must turn to the historical record for support of this claim, and even then, we cannot rely solely on objective or subjective theories and opinions. However, the evidence and experiences of people of color affirm the long history of European exploration, conquest, violence, enslavement, and oppression which put in place the system of white supremacy and institutional racial and gender inequalities we live with today.

Assuming this pre-disposition is real, western man is more aggravated than ever about their recessive genes, low birth rates, and the fear of shifting demographics which, according to the Pew Research Center's prediction that whites will be a minority in the United States in less than 30 years, a first in the country's history. This means whites are figuring out what to do to insure

26 The Iceman Inheritance, 1978 Dorset Publishing, Inc. P3-4

their survival. I suspect the upsurge in racial tensions and violence is related to what will be a new, unwelcome reality for them. For white supremacists, hate is usually the response, and guns their go-to security blankets.

In essence, white people are fighting for their lives and Black folk would be wise to know they will stop at nothing to end ours as we know it, by any means necessary. Blacks and whites who live or work in close proximity sense the growing divide. We see the handwriting on the wall with the proliferation of shootings, blatant racist attacks, and telling people of color to 'go back where they came from'. We've heard this before, but never publicly from the nation's president directing his remarks at United States citizens. Call it ignorance, apathy, or whatever you decide, but intuitively we know what this means and we know this is the sentiment of many white descendants of immigrants who migrated to the USA well after the first Africans were brought here to labor and build wealth.

Curiously, I can almost understand why those who identify as white supremacists and racists cannot reconcile with the sins of their forefathers, and feel obligated to continue their crimes against Black humanity. It is easier than bowing before the Creator and offering apologies for past offenses and vowing to go forth and sin no more. Unfortunately, acknowledging a higher spiritual power is not something people who see themselves as supreme are likely to do, and is where their religious systems fail them.

Just for fun I would like to see a study which measures anxiety levels in whites in the company of Blacks before and after they are told that science affirms the real Eve who lived over 170,000 years ago in East Africa, is the African mother of every human being alive today.[27]

****

27 The Real Eve Documentary; Journey of Man; National Genographic Project; YouTube

Archaeology and science point to Africa as the land of beginnings; the origin of humankind. There are also theories regarding the number of migrations out of Africa and which routes were taken to populate the rest of our world. Whichever paths these early migrants took out of Africa, away from the sun and nourishing plant life, they encountered changing environments and climates, which over time, changed their physical appearances. The place we today call Europe became the habitat of people we reference as Europeans or white.

Thousands of years later, in the 15th century, Europeans would return to Africa. Not in a friendly way, but seeking to exploit her natural resources and colonize her people. What began as legitimate trading in gold, ivory, textiles, and other goods later became trade in human cargo. Power and greed were the great motivators. The seeds that would result in White Supremacy/Racism were planted, germinating throughout European and American slavery and cast in stone at the Berlin Conference in 1884.

At this meeting in Germany, Spain, France, Britain, Italy, Portugal, Turkey, Austria-Hungary, Belgium, the Netherlands, Russia, Sweden-Norway, the United States and Germany took control of African land, their resources and the people. Not one African nation was invited, and none were present. After gaining independence in the 1950's, 60's, and 70's, Imperialist colonial powers continue to influence African economies, education, and the minds of her people.

****

Sigmund Freud, said to be the father of psychoanalysis and the first to use the medical term *Transference,* which describes a process in analysis or therapy which includes *Projection* and *Disassociation.* Projection is characterized by a redirection of feelings and actions from one person or group to another; while Disassociation includes symptoms of detachment of the mind from the emotional state or body, and poor memory of specific events.

Freud believed that people used psychological projection to reduce their own stress or feelings of guilt in order to protect themselves mentally. This accounts for the *blame the victim* mentality so often exhibited by whites. The oppressor is known for raping Black women and evidence of this is all around us in the lighter skin tones of many Black people, yet Black men were labeled rapists. They stole land, material resources and human resources, yet Black people are labeled thieves. Enslaved ancestors labored in the cotton, sugarcane, and tobacco fields from sun up to sun down with no pay, yet were characterized as lazy. You get the picture. The deficits of white folk were attributed to Blacks.

These labels stuck and are still used to define African Americans, except that in politically correct circles, code words such as *law and order, inner city, sense of entitlement* have replaced terms like criminals, niggers, welfare hustlers, etc. This deeply imbedded national psychosis is at the heart of America's illness which she is terrified to openly acknowledge, making healing unlikely. Although white folk in America may be *privileged,* they can never be at total peace! Lies and guilt have a way of hanging out in the background.

****

There have always been whites who crossed the color line, yet made no claim to Niggerdom. In 1926 during the Harlem Renaissance period, Carl Van Vechten, a white admirer of Black culture wrote a book entitled, *Nigger Heaven*, arousing much controversy because of its title and superficial explorations of Black life. Van Vechten would come to Harlem to live the intellectual, artistic, and party life with Black elites and return downtown to document his observations. Prominent Blacks of the time welcomed his patronage, suggesting that once you got past the title, the book was worth reading.

Van Vechten was white without apology and delighted in his honorary acceptance into the culture he enjoyed, wrote about, and documented in photos. Today's brazen white niggas are also enjoying the ride, finding greater expression among Blacks with no hard feelings. They even get to call niggers, niggas!

Having little or no experience with overt, in your face racism, our rappers, hoppers, and the nigga using crowd may think it really is different today. Being young and not fully aware, they may think today's nigga diversity will chase all of the nigger blues away and heal the soul of this nation.

Thus far, I see no evidence of healing or positive nigga empowerment. What I see is white and other non-Blacks who have not earned the right to be niggas, being entrusted with a tragic yet defiant survival history they cannot possibly understand. In actuality, these groups don't *really* care about the future of Black youth, the Black family, or Black history and legacy, yet they are being given the opportunity to work out their rebellion and nigga fantasies within a community they find tolerant, forgiving, exotic, and hip. They're in it for the good times knowing they can always opt out of Niggaville when the novelty wears off and they've had enough.

****

While there is a body of work that critiques white supremacy, racism, and white privilege as social ills, not much has been done that clinically studies why white folks do what they do in the name of nigger; why the suppression, even erasure of African contributions to world history; why they fear Black progress and why appeals to higher ethical, moral, and spiritual principles have failed to have a lasting impact on the systemic racial divide. Why? Why? Why?

Black people know the truth of why. We are living testimonies of their lies, greed, and thirst for power. And it is not uncommon for Blacks to be told that slavery, Jim Crow, and racism no longer exist and that affirmative action has leveled the playing field so '*get over it*'. Holocaust victims and their descendants receive no such reprimand.

****

Our late psychiatrist and race theorist, Dr. Frances Cress Welsing, was the first scientist in the history of Western psychiatry to psychoanalyze *White racism* instead of *victims* of racism. Dr. Welsing believes, like her mentor Neely Fuller, that in every area of people activity, white supremacy and racism are active. Her 1970 essay, *The Cress Theory of Color-Confrontation and Racism (White Supremacy)*, quickly became must reading for everyone interested in racial matters. Dr. Welsing makes three critical points:

People of color are overwhelmingly the majority population in the world; somewhere around 90% to10% for whites. Due to the biology of darker skinned people, more melanin is produced. The darker the skin color, the more melanin in their biology. Having color is the norm for humans while whiteness is a color deficiency.

Dr. Welsing states that this color deficiency and numerical deficit causes whites to envy people of color. This led to their evolving a social, political, and economic structure to give non-whites the appearance of being inferior. (*What is curious about this is the obsession whites have with tanning their skin in natural and unnatural ways at great risk to their health.)*

Fear that this numerical imbalance threatens their survival, the defensive reaction of whites was and is to impose the illusion of white supremacy and racism on people of color.

This fear gave birth to the late nineteenth century eugenics movement which advocated controlling birthrates of people of color; those who can least afford children, and those thought to be unfit. Unwanted sterilizations, birth control, and legal abortions evolved out of this philosophy.

Claims of Black genocide have also been linked to white survival. Medical experimentation, high incarceration rates; drugs, and Black on Black crime instigated by always present social and political strategies, all undermine Black communities, Black progress, and sadly, indiscriminate gangsta nigga posturing contributes to making "niggas killable, before they are killed". (Niggas to Gods; Akil)

****

Behavioral Psychologist, Dr. Edwin Nichols has developed a cross cultural thought model which he uses in diversity trainings to help workers better understand each other. He focuses on the axiology and epistemology of various ethnic/cultural groups. Axiology discusses the *highest values* of these groups; while epistemology looks at *the ways of knowing* for each group.

According to Dr. Nichols model, the highest value for Asians is group cohesion; Indigenous Americans, African Americans, Hispanics and Arabs value relationships, or person to person contact; while acquisition of the object is of the highest value for European and Euro-American groups. Dr. Nichols sites this as the reason white men, jumped from windows when the stock market crashed in 1929. The object (money) was gone and they saw no reason to live. The point to note is the difference between the highest value of Blacks and that of whites; relationships versus objects.

Epistemology for European groups or how they come to know and learn is through counting and measuring says Nichols. Statistics, reports, books and what they believe to be *proof* are needed to know things. For African Americans, symbolic imagery and rhythm informs our knowing. Living and learning through symbols, proverbs, and metaphors is how ancestors who never learned to read or write gained wisdom and foresight, enabling them to *walk by faith, and not by sight*. This is what is meant by "my soul looks back in wonder...how I got over."

Relationships and faith sustained our forefathers and mothers and supports us today in a nation invested in placing restrictions on our freedom; the kind you can count and measure. Like how many niggas have you arrested this week; how much money can we make from their incarceration? How many niggers have we mis-educated and killed, and what kind of result can we expect from this? Give me the numbers!!!!

****

History and the research of Dr. Nichols, suggests power as the main objective of white people which makes it absolutely necessary for them to be in the controlling position in their personal relationships with Blacks. Having dominion over Black lives institutionally is not enough. This accounts for whites infiltrating Niggerdom and forming alliances which have nothing to do with them wanting to be niggas, but to show that they can; an exercise in privilege and power. This is in line with whites not wanting Black people to have *anything. Nothing! Nada! Not even nigger.* Langston Hughes said. "you done taken my blues and gone" [28.] Now our nigger has been taken, had his name changed to nigga and gangsta nigga and is being mocked, sacrificed and betrayed under the misguided notion they will find favor with the enemy they mistook for a friend.

Wake up needy and naïve niggas and realize that for whites and other non-Blacks, nigga is nothing more than a coming of age sport, not a lifetime commitment. When you understand that nigga is still nigger in disguise and still offends African Americans when non-Blacks use it, you will muster up the courage to confront the imposters and demand the respect for our history knowing you

28 "You've Done Taken My Blues and Gone"; poem by Langston Hughes

will not be allowed to disrespect theirs. That won't happen until Black people make it happen. And it certainly won't happen until we stop dishonoring ourselves.

****

Calling for clinical examination of white supremacy is not an agenda item for progressive whites who express outrage and take to the streets in protest after the latest killing of an unarmed Black person or some other grievous act. They say they are for justice and equality, but stop short of calling for a national apology for slavery; reparations for the descendants of slaves, and institutionalizing genuine equality. While the Senate and House of Representatives unanimously passed Concurrent Resolution 26 in June, 2009 apologizing for slavery, this Resolution is not a Presidential Proclamation rather a formal statement which expresses the opinion of this particular Congress. It is not law.[29]

I believe our well-meaning so-called allies really would like us all to *get along* and for the nation to do better by people of color; however, a looming doubt for me is whether they actually see Blacks as equals themselves. Or, are they taking on ancestral guilt and assuaging it with topical, superficial, do-good remedies that continue to perpetuate the *Black victim/whites to the rescue* syndrome, the position whites are most comfortable with.

Too often, our white liberal compatriots exhibit their own racist subtleties and micro-aggressions when in the company of self-assertive and confident Blacks who are not their economic and/or educational subordinates. Body language provides the clue to their inner thoughts as they too, have been shaped by family beliefs and the larger society they claim they wish to change. The great abolitionist and statesman Frederick Douglass analyzed similar resentments in 1883, just eighteen years after the Emancipation Proclamation:

---

29 S.Con.Res.26 - 111th Congress (2009-2010): (Senate Congressional Resolution 26)

> "Though the colored man is no longer subject to barter and sale, he is surrounded by an adverse settlement which fetters all his movements. In his downward course he meets with no resistance, but his course upward is resented and resisted at every step of his progress. If he comes in ignorance, rags and wretchedness he conforms to the popular belief of his character, and in that character, he is welcome; but if he shall come as a gentleman, a scholar and a statesman, he is hailed as a contradiction to the national faith concerning his race, and his coming is resented as impudence."

Blacks who empower themselves with historical truths, speak on them when necessary, and reject patronization, frighten all but the sincere and committed who are willing to get down like John Brown or step up like white freedom riders and civil rights activists who non-violently and unselfishly risked and gave their lives. The primary concern of liberals who read books on how to be an anti-racist, is maintaining their privileged life-styles in safe environments free of Black anger and unrest. They also wish whites would stop behaviors which affirm their propensity for violence which justifies Black grievances. Liberals and progressives just want to be *safe!*

****

It is important to know that African American history began in the beginning, not with the forced migration of Africans to the Americas bound in chains. We are carriers of the oldest DNA and creators of the most ancient histories. Prior to archaeological evidence of high civilizations and rich traditional cultures in Africa, early European explorers, settlers writers and self-assigned historians were neither kind nor generous in their subjective judgments of Africa and her people; Gerald Massey being one of the exceptions [30].

30 Gerald Massey (May 29, 1828-October 29, 1907) was an English Egyptologist,

Having little understanding of the metaphysics of African societies, so-called scholars placed African belief systems into a European framework, interpreting African rituals and ceremonies as irrational and nonsensical. They marginalized African civilizations and timelines while embellishing their own, and conveyed these messages to the world. These are the messages that live in the collective historical memory of people around the world.

Truth is, Greek civilization, the hallmark of European civilization, did not exist until sometime around 700BC. Thanks to the research and writings of Black scholars and more objective white historians, and the always evolving internet highway, there is enough evidence which supports that centuries before their rise in the European world, Greeks and Romans went to Africa to sit at the feet of scholars in Kemet (Egypt) to learn the Kemetic Mystery Systems which included science and spirituality.

It should not be surprising that First World people, the original metaphysicians, built civilizations which defy the European's deliberate, strategized intention of denying, burying, or outright destroying evidence of African genius. This is their life's work which has become more difficult for them to get away with. We now know that much of what we were taught about European accomplishment was stolen from African invention.[31]

Unable to dispute the magnificence of ancient Nile Valley and Egyptian civilizations, those who teach our children remove Egypt from Africa to *somewhere* in the Middle East whenever they can get away with it. For these interpreters of history, it was inconceivable that Black Africans could create anything as magnificent as the Great Pyramids, the mighty Sphinx, Temples for their pharaohs and the astounding rock-hewn churches found in Ethiopia. The

---

Poet, and spiritual writer. Author of several books, his best known, "Ancient Egypt: The Light of the World is still in print.

31 Stolen Legacy; Greek Philosophy is Stolen Egyptian Philosophy by George G.M. James

population of today's Egypt is 90% Islamic Arabs and 10% Coptic and other Christian faiths. They are not the same people who inhabited Egypt when the great pyramids, impressive temples, and monuments to their pharaohs and queens were built thousands of years before the Common Era. Today's inhabitants arrived during the seventh and eighth centuries A.D.

****

I choose to believe that deep down within, the lying, cheating, and behavior which violates human decency and ridicules the underprivileged, can be a heavy burden to carry which has led to a mental imbalance. This race and fear-based illness may soon be able to be treated with a pill says an Oxford University study conducted by a team of psychologists, psychiatrists, and ethics scholars published February, 2012 in Psychopharmacology Magazine. The study used the Implicit Attitude Test – a standard test for assessing subconscious racial attitudes, and the heart medication *propranolol,* which works on parts of the brain and nervous system to reduce blood pressure, manage anxiety/panic disorders, and regulate emotional responses. Findings suggest that this pill also subconsciously lessens negative racist attitudes.

Experimental psychologist and lead author, Sylvia Terbeck said "Our results offer new evidence about the processes in the brain that shape implicit racial bias. Given the key role that such implicit attitudes appear to play in discrimination against other ethnic groups, and the widespread use of propranolol for medical purposes, our findings are also of considerable ethical interest."

A number of friends and acquaintances have no faith in a pill or any other clinical remedy. They believe hate filled speech and behaviors are deeply ingrained in the psyche and only a spiritual epiphany can provide the insight needed to appreciate the oneness of humanity and change racist attitudes.

I will add that when we consider the deletions, distortions, and omissions of African history from our basic educational process, and on-going assaults on the progress of African Americans, their findings should also be of considerable moral concern. (February, 2012 issue of Psychopharmacology Magazine for further details of study under title: *Propranolol reduces implicit Negative racial bias, Psychopharmacology DOI 10.1007/s00213-012-2657-5)*

****

Black genocide in the United States is defined as the deliberate, coordinated plan of various actions aimed at systematically killing Black people in America. Genocide in the Black world is a conversation that dates back to the 1940's which ebbs and flows with national events and their impact on Black communities.

The Civil Rights Congress, an advocacy group formed in 1948 to fight racial injustice in the criminal justice system, presented a petition to the United Nations in 1951 entitled "We Charge Genocide", requesting relief from crimes against the Negro People by the United States Government. Outlined in the paper is the historic and modern oppression of Black Americans, from lynching murders to police brutality. The paper also documented systematic inequalities in quality of life matters and health care. Here we are almost seventy years later and the charges are the same as are the disparities in health care and other social services. These major factors which create enormous stress can be linked to disease and early deaths of Black people. [32]

****

32 We Charge Genocide: The Historic Petition to the United Nations for Relief From a Crime of The United States Government Against the Negro People (New York: Civil Rights Congress, 1951), pp xi-xiii, 3-10. www.blackpast.org/global-african-hstory/primary-document

A forerunner to charges of Black genocide in America dates back to the 1890's, when a group of white men and women came together around the idea that the genetic composition of the human race needed to be improved. The mission of this Eugenics Movement was to eliminate "undesirable" traits from being passed on from generation to generation.

They were successful in getting more than 30 states to adopt compulsory sterilization laws that led to thousands of sterilizations of disabled individuals. The mentally ill; socially disadvantaged groups; and criminals were the likely candidates for extermination. Alcoholics were also thought to have inferior gene pools and were labeled unfit.

The primary methodology for preventing mentally inferior people to be born into the world was to discourage reproduction by persons having genetic defects; even sterilizing unsuspecting victims while encouraging reproduction by those deemed white and fit. Blacks and poor whites were the usual victims. It is curious to note that Margaret Sanger, founder of Planned Parenthood in 1916, was also an avid eugenicist. Promoted as an organization that supports women's rights, it was also seen as a way to lessen the Black birth rate; particularly by young, unmarried, poor Black women and girls. The majority of Planned Parenthood clinics were located in Black communities.

The Eugenics movement provided the impetus for Adolph Hitler's extermination of millions of Jews who did not meet the requirements of white, blue-eyed, blond haired Nordic or Aryan types that would make up the *master race.*

Eugenics is alive and well in today's world. For Black people, eugenics, genocide, it's all the same. We are witnesses to the criminalization of our youth; the flooding of drugs into our communities; female and male sterilizations without consent; inferior health care; inoculations and made in laboratory diseases that kill; poisoned water; medical experimentation, and possible man- made weather disasters which occur around the globe. The disproportionate number of Black children that go missing has given rise to theories that range from being kidnapped and killed for their organs for scientific and medical research to child trafficking in other countries.

****

Elder African Americans will remember the infamous Tuskegee Syphilis experiment conducted in 1932 by the U.S. Public Health Service, in conjunction with Tuskegee Institute in Macon County, Alabama. The study was called "The Tuskegee Study of Untreated Syphilis in the Negro Male". Six hundred poor and illiterate sharecroppers recruited for the Study were lied to and told they were being treated for 'bad blood', which covered several possible ailments, including syphilis and *fatigue*.

Neither the men or their families were made aware of the real purpose of the research and the very risky spinal tap-diagnostic dangers they were subject to; and they did not receive treatment to manage their illness but were offered free meals, burial insurance, and had to agree to an autopsy in order to have their funeral costs covered in the event of death. In 1932, there was no cure for syphilis and the purpose of the study was to "document" how untreated syphilis progresses in the body.

Out of the 600 participants, 399 had previous contact with syphilis, but were never told it was a deadly disease. The study was supposed to last six months, but continued for 40 years, ending in 1972. Information regarding the real purpose of the Study was withheld and new recruits suffered the same life-threatening dangers. Even though penicillin became readily available for treating the disease in 1943, it was not given to the participants. By 1947, penicillin was the standard treatment for syphilis.

The moral and ethical crime committed by the government and scientists conducting this study is that they used these men as guinea pigs and were complicit in others being infected with syphilis and the deaths of those who did not receive available treatment.

By the end of the study, it is reported that 28 persons had died from the disease, 100 persons died from related diseases and 40 wives and 19 children had been infected with syphilis. Actually, we will never know how many died or were affected by this unconscionable violation of the humanity of poor people.

In 1997, President Bill Clinton formally apologized on behalf of the government to those affected by this clearly racist experiment which was just one of many biomedical experiments and research on Black bodies carried out in U.S history and likely taking place today in laboratories and hospitals around the country, most of which never get mentioned in the media.[33]

****

During slavery, Black people suffered through untold numbers of cruel medical studies and experiments. Between1845 - 1849, J. Marion Sims, once recognized as the "father of modern gynecology," conducted multiple surgical experiments on enslaved women to treat a condition that caused vaginal pain during childbirth. He performed these procedures without anesthesia. Sims was honored for his medical accomplishments with a statue first erected in Bryant Park in the 1890's; moved to Central Park in 1934, and removed to his gravesite in Brooklyn in April, 2018 after

---

33 The Tuskegee Syphilis Study
www.cdc.gov/tuskegee/timeline.htm
Even with the end of the study and the monetary settlement, the survivors were not satisfied until President Clinton publicly apologized on May 16, 1997 for the prejudice and harmful injustices the government committed against the participants of the study

public and private re-evaluation and outcry over his controversial work in gynecology. Other statues around the country that honor dishonorable men have either come down or are under consideration for removal from their pedestals in public spaces.

****

In 1951, an African American woman from a small town outside Baltimore, Maryland went to John Hopkins Hospital complaining of pains in her stomach and unusual bleeding. She was diagnosed with cervical cancer by doctors who removed two samples of her cervix during surgery in order to conduct research – the cancerous sample and a healthy sample. Doctors observed that her cancerous cells stayed alive for longer periods of time than the other cells and regenerated themselves at a powerful rate which researchers wanted to investigate further. They named the cells HeLa for Henrietta Lacks, the name of the patient.

These powerfully regenerating cells directly contributed to breakthroughs in the fields of virology, cell culture and genetics and have created billions of dollars for the medical industry. Major advancements that would not have happened at that time without HeLa include the cure for polio, the discovery of the accurate number of human chromosomes, drugs for treating herpes, leukemia, influenza, hemophilia, and Parkinson's disease as well as the standardization of the science of cell culture. It is safe to say that Henrietta Lacks is one of the most important people in 20th century medicine; yet largely unknown outside of the medical field.

The first injustice is that Henrietta Lack's cells were removed without her permission or knowledge. She died of cervical cancer at the age of 31 on October 4, 1951 leaving five young children and family. Since her death, researchers have grown tons of her cells which are researched, analyzed, examined and will be discussed all over the world for decades to come. This was also done without the permission or knowledge of her family.

It was not until Rolling Stone magazine published an article in 1976 and the BBC produced a documentary about her life in 1996, that the remarkable story of Henrietta Lacks attracted attention. Her family discovered the importance of her life to science and the world when Rebecca Skloot published her best- selling book in 2011 entitled, "The Immortal Life of Henrietta Lacks" and a movie with the same title was produced with the help of Oprah Winfrey. No financial compensation for this unethical and immoral crime against Mrs. Lacks and her family has been offered or given by the government, scientists, or John Hopkins Hospital.

****

In 2014, a whistleblower from a leading national public health institute of the United States went public alleging the CDC did not release test results of an experimental inoculation against measles which increased the odds of Black children, especially boys, developing regressive Autism when vaccinated before the age of three. Parents of Black babies who received the vaccines were not told of the risk to their children. These are only a few examples of our government's participation in unconscionable medical acts of genocide or death against Black humanity.

Black people have always been guinea pigs for new drugs and mental and physical medical procedures. They were just niggers and no one cared. . But what Black scholars suspect is really going on rather quietly in the white scientific community, is the study of the black pigment in all nature and all humans, thought to be the chemical key to life and the brain itself; *Melanin.*

15. MELANIN: NATURE'S GENEROUS GIFT TO PEOPLE OF COLOR

"We a Baad, Black and Beautiful People"

I first became aware of the black biological substance known as melanin, also referred to as *the black dot*, at a Black History lecture in the mid-1990's. At the end of the lecture, an audience member made an announcement about an upcoming Melanin Conference where Black scientists and researchers studying melanin will speak about their findings and theories on how melanin works in the biology of people of color. He encouraged attendance so we could learn the importance of melanin, believed to be a special gift to people with dark skin.

It is well known in the scientific community and others, that the darker the skin, the more melanin one possesses. African American scholars claim that because dark skinned people have greater amounts of melanin than people who are color deficient, they also possess physical and mental attributes white supremacists and scientists disclaim, but cannot disprove.

I didn't attend the conference, nor did I conduct any further research at the time. A year or so passed before I found myself in a group conversation where melanin was brought up. No scientists were present, but opinions expressed by people who knew something about the *black dot* moved me to look closer at what our scholars are saying.

Firstly, melanin exists in all of nature; plants, animals and human beings. Melanin determines skin, hair, and eye color; and protects deeply melanated humans from harmful sun exposure which can cause skin cancer. The more melanin one has, the darker the skin, hair and eyes. Black researchers contend that melanin is also responsible for special intellectual and physical attributes which gives the darker hued a greater potential to excel intellectually and physically. This, they say, is due to their connection to the energy of the universe facilitated by melanin and the pineal gland, also known as the *third eye,* which connects richly melanated people to spirit; our divine spirit.

From my limited readings and video screenings on the subject, I make no claim to understanding all of the scientific components of melanin. What I share is from the research and writings of Black scientists and scholars in this controversial, yet scarcely publicized, area of study whose findings have global racial implications regarding the illusion of white supremacy and racism.

According to Dr. Frances Cress Welsing, people who classify themselves as white fear that because of their global minority status of approximately 10 percent white to 90 percent people of color, and their recessive genes versus dominant genes in people of color, they could be eliminated as a race of people. She draws a scientific connection between this fact and the reason the Black male is always under attack.

Welsing asserts that "white men have to destroy Black men in self defense because Black men have the potential to destroy white men genetically." Here's how: A white child can only be conceived by two white parents while Black children result from Black men with white women; Black women with white men, and two Black parents. The reason simply put is the genes of heavily melanated people are dominant while white people's genes are recessive. When whites and Blacks produce offspring, Black genes will dominate. This dominant/recessive science indicates a kind of power whites cannot compete with and begs the question of which race is truly superior if there is such a thing. It also suggests that whites are literally fighting for their lives.

Going back to the oppression of slavery and our ancestors being forbidden to learn to read, write and express their gifts freely, up until today, the ruling class is fighting to survive and keep alive their illusion of superiority. This makes it necessary for them to keep African Americans out of mainstream competition. History shows that when allowed in, we break records and reach high levels of success in all areas of human activity. An underlying envy suggests that white folks know that Black people are wired differently; that we possess special gifts and that they must deny us equal access. Simply put, white folk cannot do what we do?

White supremacists would have us believe that Black people are inferior based on pseudo scientific arguments. In actuality, their exclusionary behavior sends an entirely different message. Superior people have no need to lie, cheat, suppress, distort, and steal the accomplishments of others, or deny equality and justice to those who possess an abundance of Mother Nature's special gift.

As African descendants, we are not only rich in melanin, but are also the inheritors of emotional resilience and spiritual fortitude. Our ancestral land is blessed by the warmth of the Sun, an abundance of natural resources, and the wonders and mysteries of nature are all around, reinforcing deep bonds with the God of our understanding. We cannot be broken!

Senior Research Chemist, Carol Barnes, author of *Melanin: The Chemical Key to Black Greatness,* says this:

- Melanin refines the nervous system in such a way that messages from the brain reach other areas of the body most rapidly in Black people; the original people.

- Melanin is the neuro-chemical basis for what is called SOUL in Black people

- Blacks excel in athletics and other areas of people activity once road blocks are challenged and removed.

- Melanin gives humans the ability to FEEL because it is the absorber of all frequencies of energy.

Dr. Barnes also found that "drug abuse by Blacks is more likely because Melanin is responsible for Blacks becoming addicted faster and staying addicted longer. We don't have to be brilliant to see why drugs are deliberately placed in Black communities.

There are numerous other effects of melanin in the biology of darker skinned people scientists are researching. The pineal gland, also known as the third eye, and the seat of the soul is thought to work closely with melanin to produce deep spiritual insights and broaden our understanding of the human experience. Black people who understand the gift of their abundance of melanin do not think of themselves as inferior to whites. We know the greatness of our ancestors and all they have given to the world others take credit for.

Melanin: Key to Freedom and other works by psychiatrist, historian, and melanin/pineal gland scholar Dr. Richard King, and the lectures on melanin and the pineal gland by Dr. Ann Brown, are eye-opening and easy to understand. Their white counterparts hide information in highly technical concepts and language only those with science backgrounds can understand. Dr. Karl Maret who is white discusses The Science of Melanin in a You Tube video and he never mentions Black people.

****

According to Dr. King, the central role Melanin plays in Black bodies has been "suppressed to maintain the mythological inferiority of Blacks...and the defensive clinging to whiteness as some token of superiority." Dr. King states further that the "*superiority complex* of white people is a defense mechanism and a mask for their deepest *inferiority complex* which they project on to people of color." Dr. Timothy O. Moore, Dr. Leonard Jeffries, Professor James Small, Dr. Laila Africa, Bobby Hemmit, are among other scholars also studying and sharing their findings on melanin. You can access their scholarship on the You Tube (*University)* channel.

As the field of melanin researchers grows, we are learning a great deal more about the benefits of this *black dot.* Yet, in keeping with white supremacy and racist thought, an entry in Wikipedia, the on-line encyclopedia, states, the "Melanin theory that a higher level of melanin is the cause of intellectual and physical superiority of dark-skinned people and provides them with supernatural powers" is a racist, pseudoscientific claim in Afrocentrism". But they can't prove it.

Of course, we know Wikipedia offers limited scholarship, but the evidence speaks for itself. Question the evidence not the opinions of our detractors. a) Why did European conquerors, archaeologists, anthropologists, historians, scientists, educators, and all who classify themselves as *white,* agree to hide, minimize, distort, delete, and steal the history of Africans wherever they are in the world; and why, when given the opportunity to seriously compete, Black people excel in all areas of people activity.

As trite as this may seem, we know that Black folks have earthly rhythm and the rhythm of the universe coursing through our veins. We speak in tongues, nuance, and knowing looks. We are wizards who make magic and call up supernatural powers in times of need. We got style, moves, and we keep time with the beat. It's no wonder white folks are intrigued by us; and they have got to wonder how our ancestors survived the beat downs and still raised their children even after nigger became a word in their limited vocabulary.

The racial divide that plagues this nation has been stoked by #45 who many felt was unfit to serve as president. He was only the third president in the history of the United States to be impeached for abuse of power; twice.

****

The threat of people of color soon becoming the majority population; the rise in Black consciousness regarding America's agenda for Black lives; the research and teachings of our scholars which furthers our understanding of our status as the original, great people of the world, and all that is possible for us when we do fully understand, are frightening prospects for our fairer-skinned cousins.

While it may appear we are in a bleak period during the current political and racial climate, young people may not know we have been at these crossroads before and have kept the faith that we would rise again. This time, when we rise, we will claim our crowns and be the NEGAS we are destined to be. And when we rise, we need all of our soldiers, comrades, and niggas; gangstas included, to rise up together.

Look at the evidence of Black achievement in spite of hundreds of years of being oppressed. Do your own melanin research and draw your own conclusions about this precious black dot and be proud and appreciative of whichever hue of Black you represent and know you have been given a special gift, carry dominant genes within your biology, and have a divine connection to the universal ALL.

In honoring generations of ancestors who moved us forward, my commitment is to use what's in my hands to bring information to our young people that will raise their racial self-esteem in this time of compromised morals and values.

16. UNTIL LIONS HAVE THEIR HISTORIANS

If you really want to do something, you'll find a way
If you don't, you'll find an excuse

The real questions to be answered are; how can African Americans properly assign the word nigger so that we do not forget or gloss over its sordid history; respect its affectionate, fraternal, and supportive role in Black life; render it powerless when meant as an assault or unfriendly distraction; and put an end to friendly use among other ethnic groups, and adhere to higher standards for its use by African Americans and Africans in the Dispora.

When higher standards are set, the word itself will take its rightful place in our lives and places of learning. If spic, honky, cracker, redneck, greaseball, gringo, mickey, hebe, chink, kyke, and all other disparaging ethnic references are not blatantly and carelessly used, we should not allow *nigger*, the most controversial of them all, to be disrespectfully bandied about. Don't be fooled by the changed spelling. The Black tax our ancestors paid and we continue to pay is too high.

Truth is, there have always been discerning African Americans who have not allowed racist interpretations to obliterate their own perceptions of the word. They know its history; the good, the bad, and the ugly; they do not abuse it, and have no intention of eliminating it from their vocabulary. They have already claimed power, choosing their own characterizations and fraternal understanding, placing it in the power position, using the word for emphasis as only brothers can do. These are Negas expressing as insightful and wise niggers who are not the subject of this writing.

****

There is an African proverb which says, "until lions have their own historians, tales of the hunt will always glorify the hunter." This piece of wisdom should not need an explanation. We know who wrote and controlled the narrative of Africa and her people throughout the Dispora and the effectiveness of their erasure and misrepresentation of Black histories.

Today we have our own scholars and historians researching our truths and exposing the lies, distortions, and omissions from the global historical record. Sleeping lions are waking and taking their stand with brothers and sisters who are prepared to wage cultural and spiritual warfare based in our African knowledge foundation which Dr. Karenga tells us means "understanding and appreciating values which honors nature, culture, ancestors, family, and history".

African Americans are descendants of an ancient people, "as old as the world, and older than the flow of human blood in human veins" (Rivers; Langston Hughes) . As America continues to grapple with her karma and unravel before the world, white supremacists and racists are desperate, and the killings are escalating. This may sound like a ridiculous question, but, 'can they kill us all?' Or put us all in jail? Will they go that far?

Meanwhile, African Americans are looking more to our Higher Power for the spiritual healing and redemption of our people. Our faith, hope, and sheer will to persevere and reinvent ourselves guarantees our victory. The material power of our adversaries cannot compete with the spiritual and supernatural power inherited from the ancients. We have only to claim and accept our power.

Change is not always easy, and it takes time to become comfortable with transitions. Learning more about our history and telling more of our own stories gives us the confidence needed to take on what lies before us.

Hip-hoppers, rappers, gangstas, in fact everyone will benefit from this new model for referencing, defining and using the term nigga with respect. Just as nigus, negus, negro, negre transitioned into nigger, we can change nigger(nigga) back to Negus. Greater challenges we have met and conquered. Greater miracles we have performed. As I've said, it's all in the pronunciation and interpretation.

Let's remember the prophetic words of the Honorable Marcus Mosiah Garvey who declared during his imprisonment, that "You may have caged the lion, but his cubs are running loose." Be the cubs becoming lions with the purpose of continuing the changes in the world already begun.

17. CROSSING OVER JORDAN

"When we get to the other side, freedom from mental slavery will be waiting!"

From the days of African American enslavement up until the 1950's and 60's, Black consciousness for the masses meant understanding who we were in relationship to the larger American society and working within the system to gain respect and equal rights. We could not enjoy the kind of freedom the privileged class enjoyed, but we managed to make family, make progress, and enjoy good times.

Education was stressed as a stepping stone to a higher standard of living and forward movement as a people; emphasizing always that it was the one thing the white man could not take away. Elders in our religious and social institutions charged us with being *credits to our race* and furthering our cause for dignity and respect. For many of us entering adulthood in the 1960's a high school diploma and the prospect of clerical/secretarial work or a civil service job with the government were respectable ambitions for working class Black women. For men with no skills or crafts such as carpentry, plumbing, electrician, or masonry; civil service, doormen, elevator operators, chauffeurs, and other uniformed service jobs was considered decent employment. If fortunate enough to go to college right out of high school, as important as good grades was good character; being a good role model, and paving a way for those who would come after. *Make your family proud* was the anthem ingrained in our psyche.

For the most part, Black people kept their heads down and their mouths shut, enduring second class status, yet taking small steps towards better jobs and living conditions. The Black Church served as our spiritual and social refuge and platform for our leaders brave enough to challenge the system and take on the most dangerous of our collective goals; self-determination. They knew freedom was not free; and that death was often the price they would have to pay, but they forged ahead thinking only of creating a better life for posterity. They did not allow fear of the unknown to keep them stuck in the familiar.

Malcolm X, Dr. Martin Luther King, Medgar Evers, are the better known leaders killed because they spoke truth to power.There were so many other unsung heroes who were beaten, jailed, and murdered attempting to move this country towards its professed promise of liberty and justice for all.

African leaders who pressed for reforms in their nations were also assassinated while despot rulers exploited and restricted freedoms of their citizenry with the help of countries like the USA. Patrice Lumumba of the Congo; Chris Hani of South Africa, and Thomas Sankara are among those leaders who were assassinated or killed because they pressed for reforms in their governments. This speaks to the global nature of the challenges African people face wherever we are.

****

Civil Rights legislature and anti-poverty programs enacted in the 60's provided some legal remedies in discrimination cases and elevated some African Americans out of borderline poverty into the middle-class.

African Americans who were educated and well-off dating back to the 1800's, survived in their own economic and social bubbles and managed to live between Black and white worlds in America unnoticed and without incident . Many of our doctors, lawyers, and Indian Chiefs are in this class and represent a certain professionalism and stability in our communities, even though they may be less prone to publicly vocalize any discontent with the system. The turbulence and civil unrest of the 1960's had an impact serious enough for the government to neutralize and put restraints in place that would not allow another movement of its radical intensity.

By the 1980's, large scale infiltration of highly addicted drugs into Black and Latino communities brought crime, despair and a growing hopelessness. This state of affairs led to deliberate tracking of drug victims into our system of legal enslavement, the prison industrial complex where nigga mentalities are honed and made ready to wreak havoc upon re-entry into society. How ironic that the 13th Amendment to the Constitution, the one that *freed the slaves*, is the same amendment containing the loophole which allows for legal slavery. (See note 4 for full reading of this amendment).

****

Greater competition for jobs and rising costs for higher education collided with challenges to affirmative action in American universities and corporations. Here again, African Americans faced threats to their advancement and acceptance in American life. This is where we see the residual effects of slavery play out.

So, what is the point of all that has been said; and why should we care. For those who do not care, little difference will be made in their lives. The blueprint for continued criminalization and incarceration of our young men does not matter; and that additional strategies for Black genocide is on the books, is of little interest. For those who do care, there is work to be done; work we gotta do if we want to cross over Jordan.

All niggas are not rappers with record deals and nouveau riche lifestyles. This leaves regular hood niggas and hip-hoppers buying into a gangsta culture that feels good and offers temporary relief from the weight of surviving in marginal communities where poverty and cynical mentalities lean on each other. I wonder if they suspect how easy they make it for politicians and police to do their dirty work of implementing what appears to be a national mandate to criminalize and imprison Black youth; kill them when possible; and render them powerless with little hope for their future, all in the name of nigger, the old fashioned kind with a new spelling. It's happening as I write.

****

Understanding that language and word definitions change over time, we must still be discerning when it comes to words full of histories that should be authentically remembered. Creating a new nigga, a white nigga, or any other questionable version of nigger is not redemptive or beneficial nor does it empower Black people with whom it is associated as no one thinks of the imposters as *real* niggas. They themselves know they will be forgiven their wayward behaviors when they are ready to return to strong cultural and family roots where some things are sacred and honored as such; where home affairs are not discussed in public venues or on public platforms, where going everyday public with ethnic slurs associated with their group is not up for consideration. These imposters should have never been allowed to take up residency in the Black inner sanctum with no qualifications for occupancy. They need to be evicted.

****

In 1903, WEB DuBois said that 'the problem of the color line' was the problem of the 20th century." Over a hundred years later, we're still wrestling with this problem. My thought is, if African Americans and people of color are destined to always be referenced as niggers, we will determine the type of Negas we will be in the world. If we believe that 'black lives matter', we must believe that dignity, integrity, and respect for Black lives also matters.

****

Unlike the Black press which has always reported on concerns and triumphs of African Americans in all aspects of our lives, mainstream media primarily reports on Black life in three categories; crime, entertainment and sports. It is this shameless disregard for a fuller telling of American African accomplishments that led Dr. Carter G. Woodson to begin publishing the Journal of Negro History in 1916, and to create Negro History Week in 1926, becoming a month-long celebration in 1976. He realized that it was up to African Americans to tell and document their own stories of triumphs and victories and point out the omissions in the historical narrative written and told by others.

Much of American history was written by whites who claimed they discovered or created what was already there. When Columbus *discovered* America and the European world celebrated, the indigenous people living and honoring the land, nature, and family were not considered. The native people welcomed the newcomers and shared their bountiful harvest. The newcomers repaid their generosity with greed, broken treaties, and forced eviction from their land.

****

During slavery, America was the only country where it was against the law for enslaved people to learn to read or write. Harriet Tubman had no book learning; neither did Sojourner Truth. But this did not stop them from speaking and taking action against the system which held them in bondage. Frederick Douglass escaped from slavery; Booker T. Washington became free when the Emancipation Proclamation was ratified, and Carter G. Woodson, son of slaves and the second African American to earn a doctorate degree from Harvard University, are just a sampling of African Americans, handicapped by the law, who went on to high achievement, impacting history and the lives of African Americans in profound ways.

In the tradition of our scholars, educators, and statesmen who managed to rise above the oppression of their day, write books and speak out in order to keep Black people informed, growing numbers of Africans, African Americans, and Africans in the Dispora are researching and filling in the missing pages of history. And it is our responsibility to learn this history and teach it to our youth. Education is a weapon and an important act of resistance.

Black Lives Matter and other social justice movements are setting examples and have laid our work out. Stopping the cycle of cultural ignorance and preparing ourselves to combat the new generation of nigger haters being raised by white supremacists is a charge we cannot ignore. What this new generation of racists will realize is that the racial divide is as old as the country. And, as the old Negro gospel song laments "so wide, we can't get around it; so high we can't get over it, and so low, we can't get under it. We must come in at the door." And we will come thru the door cloaked in our full African Holy Ghost armor, ready to take on what lies ahead. So, people get ready! Take up your Nega crowns and place them upon your proud and enlightened Black heads. It's time to "cross over Jordan".

****

THE GOSPEL TRUTH

"IF THERE IS A JUST GOD,
WE'RE GOING TO PAY FOR THIS"

Thomas Jefferson

"GOD GAVE NOAH THE RAINBOW SIGN NO
MORE WATER, THE FIRE NEXT TIME"

James Baldwin

CPSIA information can be obtained
at www.ICGtesting.com
Printed in the USA
BVHW081953041021
618074BV00001B/2

9 781647 494872